MASSAGE THERAPY IN AYURVEDA

Pañcakarma Therapy of Ayurveda Series No. 1

MASSAGE THERAPY IN AYURVEDA

VAIDYA BHAGWAN DASH

CONCEPT PUBLISHING COMPANY, NEW DELHI 110059

ISBN 81-7022-380-6

First Published 1992
Reprinted 1994, 1998

Published and Printed by
Ashok Kumar Mittal
Concept Publishing Company
A/15-16, Commercial Block, Mohan Garden
NEW DELHI 110059 (INDIA)

Lasertypeset by
Microtech Advance Printing Systems (Pvt.) Ltd.
H-13, Bali Nagar
NEW DELHI 110015

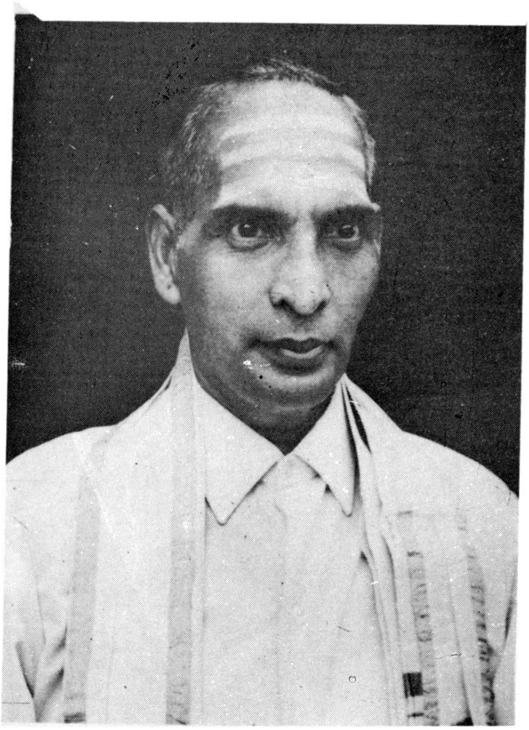

Late Astavaidyan

Vaịaskara N.S. Mooss

who through his untiring efforts
propagated the knowledge of Ayurveda in general and
Ayurvedic massage therapy in particular in India and abroad.

PREFACE

Ayurveda is the rich store house of time tasted and effective recipes for the treatment of several obstinate and otherwise incurable diseases. More important than these recipes are the specialised therapies which, while curing such diseases strengthen the immunity system in the body and thus help in the prevention of diseases and preservation as well as promotion of Positive health. Not withstanding the phenomenal progress of modern medicine very little is achieved so far in the field of evolving measures for the promotion of this Positive health. These specialised therapies in ayurvedic parlance, are called *Pañcakarma*. It is no wonder therefore, that scientists and physicians in India and abroad are evincing deep interest in this classical form of ayurvedic treatment.

If one opens any chapter on the treatment of diseases in Ayurvedic classics, the first point which will strike his attention is the description of the *Pañcakarma* measures for that ailment, recipes coming next thereafter. *Pañcakarma* therapy primarily aims at cleansing the body of its accumulated impurities and nourishing the tissues. Once this is achieved, it becomes very easy to rejuvenate these tissues and prevent the process of ageing. The span of life is thus prolonged and the individual leads a disease free old age. He becomes capable of serving the society with his accumulated experience without any mental disability and physical decay. Even if he succumbs to a disease, this *Pañcakarma* therapy, if administered appropriately, makes his body more receptive to other remedies and those recipes produce the curing effect even when administered is smaller dose and for less number of days. In rural India, oil massage before bath is regularly practised even now and it is given the status of a religious ritual inasmuch as bath without oil massage is considered inauspicious. Unfortunately, because of historical reasons, this classical form of massage treatment went out of practice, and in its place, only recipes were used both for the prevention and cure of diseases. But fortunately for us, the ayurvedic physicians of South India kept this classical tradition alive, and in view of the importance and therapeutic utility both for healthy persons as well as patients, its practice is now being revived in other parts of India and even abroad. The term *Pañcakarma* literally means five (*pañca*) specialised therapies (*karma*). The therapies which are included under this collective term are as follows:

(1) *Vamana karma* or Emetic therapy.
(2) *Virecana karma* or Purgation therapy.
(3) *Nirūha karma* or a therapy administered through medicated enema containing decoction of drugs, among others.
(4) *Anuvāsana karma* or a therapy administered through medicated enema containing medicated oils, among others.
(5) *Nasya karma* or Inhalation therapy.

Suśruta's school which deals with surgery includes *rakta-mokṣaṇa karma* or blood-letting therapy in the place of *nasya karma* or Inhalation therapy.

It is necessary at this state to make it clear that these therapies do not imply simple administration of emesis, purgation, enema or nasal drops as is conventionally understood. Elaborate methods are described for the preparation of therapies, their methods of administration, preparation of the individual prior to the administration of these therapies and the management of the patient (or the healthy person) after the therapy is administered.

Prior to the administration of these therapies, the body of the patient is to be suitably prepared and the therapeutic measures used for this purpose are called *pūrva karma* or preparatory therapies. These are two in number as follows:

(a) *Snehana karma* or Oleation therapy; and
(b) *Svedana karma* or Fomentation therapy.

Snehana karma or Oleation therapy is administered in two different ways, viz., externally (*bāhya snehana*) and internally (*ābhyantara snehana*). The external form is given through different types of massage with the help of ordinary or medicated oil and powders and pastes of medicinal plants as well as animal products including metallic preparations. To keep the body healthy and to prevent as well as cure manifested diseases, this massage should be done every day either over the whole body or over different specific parts of the body.

During the course of time some special massage therapies have been developed in ayurveda and are still in practice in certain pockets of South India. These special massage therapies cause both oleation and fomentation of the body. Apart from curing some of the obstinate and otherwise incurable diseases, these special massage therapies help in rejuvenating the body. If used periodically, they prevent the ageing process while simultaneously preventing the manifestation of diseases. Thus, massage, apart from its utility as a preparatory measure for other therapies included under *Pañca karma* is a specialised therapy in its own merit.

In addition to *Navarakizhi* and *Pizhichil* which are described in this work, there are several other similar therapies like *Anna lepana* which are not described here for brevity. But *Dhārā* or pouring oil, ghee, butter-milk and milk over the forehead in drops and *Śirobasti* or keeping oil over the head are two important forms of massage therapy. These are described in this work in view of their excellent therapeutic effects.

In subsequent volumes of this *Pañcakarma* Therapy of Ayurveda series, we shall bring out other therapeutic measures under this category. The present volume, as the title indicates, is devoted to massage only.

While administring Massage therapy, the patient has to be careful about his food and drinks. Different types of oil, milk, milk-products and water are required for the preparation of recipes and for food as well as drinks of the patient. The Physician should be well aquainted with the properties of these ingredients as described in Ayurveda. This will enable him to select the appropriate ingredients for his patient. This information is provided in Appendix-I.

Medicated oils are generally used for different types of massage–both for the routine massage and for massage as a specialised therapy. The method of manufacturing these medicated oils and their recipes are given in Appendix-III. Abbreviations used for the parts of plants included in these recipes are described in Appendix-II.

At the end, the Bibliography and an Index to technical terms used in the main text only with explanation of some of these terms is given for the convenience of reference.

This work is meant to simply aquaint the reader about this specialised therapy of Ayurveda. The author will feel amply satisfied if this could incite interest of physicians and scientists on this subject.

BHAGWAN DASH

INDO-ROMANIC EQUIVALENTS OF DEVANAGARI

अ	a	च	ca	भ	bha
आ	ā	छ	cha	म	ma
इ	i	ज	ja	य	ya
ई	ī	झ	jha	र	ra
उ	u	त्र	ña	ल	la
ऊ	ū	ट	ṭa	व	va
ऋ	ṛ	ठ	ṭha	श	śa
ए	e	ड	ḍa	ष	ṣa
ऐ	ai	ढ	ḍha	स	sa
ओ	o	ण	ṇa	ह	ha
औ	au	त	ta		
अं	ṁ/ṃ	थ	tha		
अः	ḥ	द	da		
क	ka	ध	dha		
ख	kha	न	na		
ग	ga	प	pa		
घ	gha	फ	pha		
ड.	ṅa	ब	ba		

CONTENTS

Preface 7
Indo-Romanic Equivalents of Devanāgarī 11
List of Figures 15

1. Introduction 17
What is health. —Therapeutical necessities, —Classification of Therapies.
2. *Snehana* or Oleation therapy 19
Classification of Ayurvedic therapies.
3. Regular Massage 21
Jarā or Ageing process, —*Śrama* or Fatigue, —*Vāta Roga* or Nervous disorders, —*Dṛṣṭi* or Eye-sight, —*Puṣṭi* or Nourishment of the tissue elements, —*Āyuṣ* or Longevity, —*Svapna* or Sleep, —*Dārḍhya* or Sturdiness, —Metaphoric illustrations, —Massage should be done Regularly, —Time of Oil Massage, —Massage and Physical exercises, —Auspicious days, —Inauspicious days, —Massage in Prohibited days, —Signs and symptoms of appropriate Oleation therapy, —Contra-indications, —Modes of administering Massage therapy, —Massage over the whole or parts of the body.
4. Head massage (*Śiro'bhyaṅga*) 30
5. Filling the ears with oil (*Karṇa Pūraṇa*) 31
6. Massage over the soles of feet (*Pādābhyaṅga*) 32
Time taken to permeate through different tissues, —Other methods of massage.
7. *Udvartana* or Unction 34
Benefits of *udvartana*, —Recipe for *udvartana*.
8. *Udgharṣaṇa* or Rubbing the body with powders 36

9. Different types of fat used in Massage therapy 37
Properties of different types of fat, —ghee, —oil, —muscle fat, —bone marrow, —comparison of properties, —oil of oil-seeds, —Properties of sesame-oil, —Different types of oil used for different specific purposes.
10. Special Massage Therapies 44
11. *Piṇḍasveda* or *Navarakizhi* 45
Preparation of decoction and pudding, Cloth-pieces, —Preparation of boluses, —Application of oil, —Need for oil massage, —Protection of eyes, —Massage table, —Position of Body, —Bath, —Course of Therapy.
12. *Kāyaseka* or *Pizhichil* 58
13. *Śirodhārā* or Pouring oil etc., over the head 61
14. *Taila dhārā* 62
Manufacture of medicated oil.
15. *Dugdha dhārā* 66
16. *Takra dhārā* 68
17. *Śirobasti* (Oleation of the head) 69
Method of Administration, —Therapeutic utility.
18. Precautions and Regimens 71
Preparation of the patient, —Water for drinking and bath, —Conduct and regimens, —Diet, —Importance of proper bowel movement, —Drinks, —Sleep, —Clothing, —Exercise, —Study, —Fresh air, —Friends and attendants, —Bath, —Other regimens, —Suitable time, —Course of treatment, —Suppression of natural urges (*Vega-rodha*).

Appendix - I 85
Properties of important ingredients used in Massage Therapy
Appendix - II 119
Abbreviations used for parts of plants in recipes
Appendix - III 120
Pharmaceutical process for manufacturing medicated oil and recipes
Appendix - IV 167
Vegetable drugs and their botanical names.

Bibliography 188
Index 189

LIST OF FIGURES

1. *Piṇḍa* or Medicated Rice bolus being tied with a string 47

2. Four *Piṇḍas* or Medicated rice boluses being kept ready before massage 47

3. Traditional Massage Table without Pedestal 49

4. Measurements of the Traditional Massage Table 49

5. Modern Massage Table with a Pedestal 51

6. The patient in lying position. The head is traditionally covered with the paste of *āmalakī* and tied with a banadage before massage 53

7. The massage of chest. *Piṇḍa* is kept down. Because the patient is emaciated, to begin with, the massage is done with the paste squeezed out of the paste 54

8. Massage of the abdomen 54

9. Massage of the back 55

10. Vessel for *Dhārā* Therapy (Traditional) 63

11. *Dhārā* of the head 64

12. *Dhārā* can be given to only a part of the body 64

1

INTRODUCTION

Ayurveda literally means "the Science of Life". For the promotion of positive health and prevention and cure of diseases, it is in practice in India and its neighbouring countries since time immemorial. "Health", according to ayurveda is not merely the freedom from diseases. A person is to be treated as healthy only when his mind, sense organs and the soul are in the state of perfect of equilibrium to endow happiness. In addition, the body should be free from diseases. Ayurveda lays a lot of emphasis on the preservation and promotion of positive health in addition to the prevention and cure of diseases. Therefore, several therapeutic measures, both for patients and healthy persons are prescribed in this system of medicine.

What is Health ?

According to Suśruta (*Suśruta Saṃhitā : Sūtra :* 16 : 44) – a person having the equilibrium of *doṣas* (*vāyu, pitta* and *kapha*, which are responsible for the functioning and mal-functioning of different organs of the body), *agnis* (enzymes responsible for the digestion and metabolism), *dhātus* (tissue elements constituting the structure of the individual's body) and *malas* (waste products which are eliminated from the body) and happiness of the soul, senses and the mind, is to be treated as "healthy".

Therapeutical Necessities

As a physiological process, the body of an individual undergoes several changes during different stages of life, during the different parts of the day and night and during different seasons. The body has the inbuilt power of resistance to overcome some of these minor changes. But, if these changes are significant, then even a healthy person suffers from diseases. To promote this inbuilt power of resistance in the body, to overcome different changes, and to correct a malady if it has already got manifested, several therapeutic measures in the forms of drugs, diet, drinks, regimens and specialised therapies, are described in Ayurvedic works and prescribed by physicians.

Classification of Therapies

Therapies are broadly classified into two categories, namely, (1) *Apatarpaṇa* or Depleting Therapy and (2) *Santarpaṇa* or Nourishing Therapy. The latter category i.e. Nourishing Therapy is further sub-devided into 3 groups, namely:–

(1) *Bṛṃhaṇa* (which promotes corpulance of the body);
(2) *Snehana* (Oleation Therapy); and
(3) *Stambhana* (which inhibits un-natural secretions and excretions from the body).

A detailed classification of ayurvedic therapies is given in the chart in the next chapter. It will be seen from that the *snehana* or oleation therapy plays an important role in ayurvedic mode of treatment. It is done by massage and application of oil, etc., over the skin of the body which is called *bāhya snehana* (external oleation therapy).

2

SNEHANA OR OLEATION THERAPY

Oleation Therapy plays a significant role for:

(1) the preservation and promotion of positive health; and
(2) the prevention and cure of diseases.

This Oleation Therapy is administered to a person in two different ways, as follows:

(1) External application in the form of massage (*abhyaṅga*); and
(2) Internal administration (*snehapāna*).

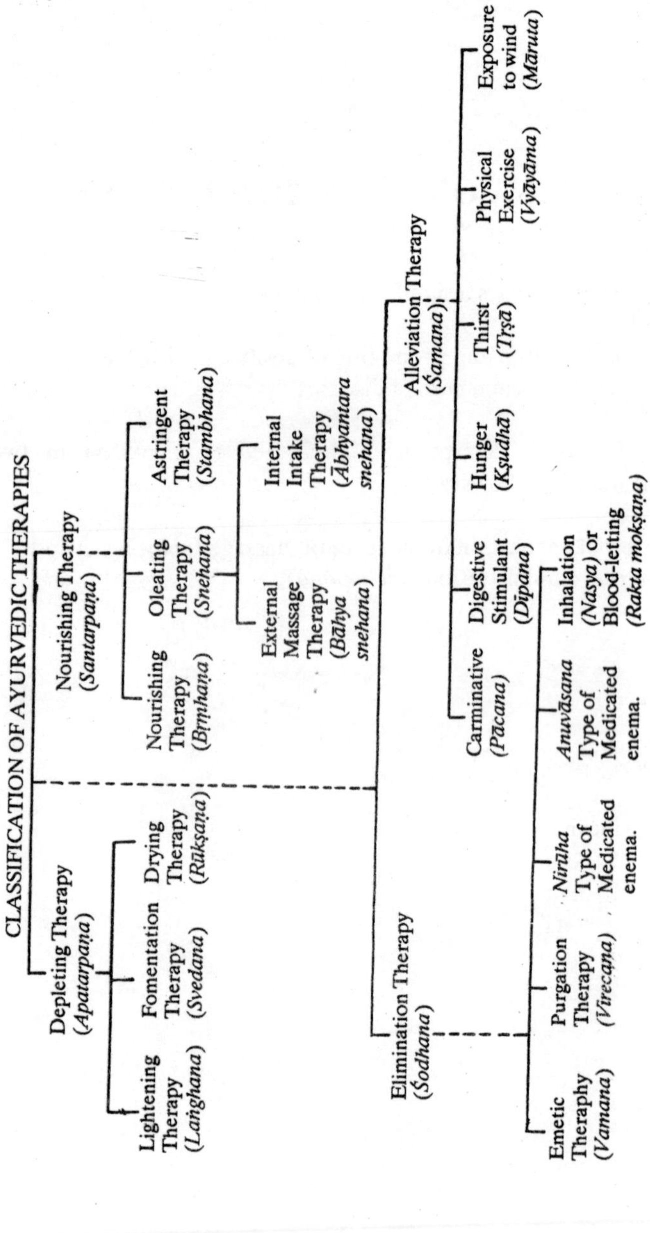
CLASSIFICATION OF AYURVEDIC THERAPIES
Depleting Therapy (Apatarpaṇa)
Nourishing Therapy (Santarpaṇa)
Lightening Therapy (Laṅghana)
Fomentation Therapy (Svedana)
Drying Therapy (Rūkṣaṇa)
Nourishing Therapy (Bṛṃhaṇa)
Oleating Therapy (Snehana)
Astringent Therapy (Stambhana)
External Massage Therapy (Bāhya snehana)
Internal Intake Therapy (Ābhyantara snehana)
Elimination Therapy (Śodhana)
Alleviation Therapy (Śamana)
Emetic Theraphy (Vamana)
Purgation Therapy (Virecaṇa)
Nirūha Type of Medicated enema.
Anuvāsana Type of Medicated enema.
Inhalation (Nasya) or Blood-letting (Rakta mokṣaṇa)
Carminative (Pācana)
Digestive Stimulant (Dīpana)
Hunger (Kṣudhā)
Thirst (Tṛṣā)
Physical Exercise (Vyāyāma)
Exposure to wind (Māruta)

3

REGULAR MASSAGE

According to Vāgbhaṭa (*Aṣṭāṅga Hṛdaya : Sūtra* : 2 : 7-8), a person, with a view to preserving and promoting his positive health and preventing and curing his diseases, should use massage therapy every day. It has the following specific attributes:

(i) It prevents and corrects ageing process (*jarā*);
(ii) It helps a person to overcome fatigue (*śrama*) because of routine hard work in life;
(iii) It prevents and corrects disorders caused by the affliction of the nervous system (*vāta*);
(iv) It promotes eye-sight (*dṛṣṭi prasāda*);
(v) It helps nourishment (*puṣṭi*) of the body;
(vi) It promotes longevity (*āyuṣ*) of an individual;
(vii) It helps the individual to get sleep (*svapna*); and
(viii) It promotes sturdiness (*dārḍhya*) of the individual.

I. Jarā or Ageing Process

Death is inevitable. But, untimely death and the diseases caused because of the ageing process can be easily prevented. Apart from the greying of hair and wrinkling of the skin, the ageing process affects eye-sight, power of hearing, conditions of teeth, the power of digestion, movement of bowels and sleep. During old age, the bones undergo changes giving rise to osteo-arthritis; the vertibral column becomes weak and the discs in between the two vertibrae get either calcified resulting in the stiffness or get destroyed resulting in slip-disc and pain in the back and spondylitic changes in the vertibrae, arresting movement and increasing stiffness of the body giving rise to pain and giddiness. A person in his old age suffers from Parkinson's disease (Paralysis agitans). The muscles of the heart and arteries lose their flaxibility giving rise to heart diseases, arteriosclerosis and high blood pressure.

Because of changes in the arteries, supply of normal blood is affected giving rise to senile degeneration of brain tissues. During the old age, persons therefore, suffer from sleeplessness and lack of memory power. If there is a rupture of the arteries in the brain because of the high blood pressure, a person may get paralysis. All these and other changes/diseases of the old age could be prevented and cured, if these are already manifested, by the regular use of massage therapy.

II. Śrama or Fatigue

During the physical exercise or ordinary physical work, some metabolic products get accumulated in the neuro-muscular junctions leading to fatigue. If the neuro-muscular junctions are kept clean, and if both the nerve and the muscle tissues are toned up, then the person could avert fatigue in spite of hard work and physical exercise. This is possible through massage therapy. If a person is already fatigued, then this could be corrected quickly and easily by appropriate massage.

III. Vāta Roga or Nervous Disorders

All the physical and psychic functions of the individual are regulated by three basic factors, viz., *vāyu, pitta* and *kapha. Vāyu* or *vāta* regulates all the sensatory and motor functions of the nervous system. *Pitta* regulates all the enzymatic reactions including digestion and metaboism in the body. *Kapha* or *śleṣmā* keeps the body organs together thereby facilitating their harmoneous functioning. The activities of *pitta* and *kapha* are regulated by *vāyu*, and therefore, this *vāyu* plays the most important role in the creation, sustenance, decay and destruction of the body. Similarly, it exercises considerable influence on the functioning of the mind. Therefore, for the individual to be healthy and happy this *vāyu* should he kept in the state of equilibrium. Massage therapy helps in the promotion and regulation of the proper functioning of this *vāyu* or nervous activities.

IV. Dṛṣṭi or Eye-Sight

Eye plays an important role in the normal activities of the individual. Because of its misuse like constant study in improper light and wrong position, reading exceedingly small letters, watching television for a long time, exposure to dazzling light, constant gazing at luminous bodies, solar eclipse and lunal eclipse, exposing the head to excess to heat, taking head bath with hot water and taking pungent and ununctuous food and drinks, a person suffers from impairment of vision. Besides, because of ageing process, a person in old age suffers from cataract, myopia and malfunctioning of the optic nerve. Because of wrong diet and regimen a person at times falls victim to invalidating eye-ailments like retinitis pigmentosa, detached ratina and atrophy of the optic nerve. Even the common constipation may give rise to several eye disorders including impairment of the vision as a result of which at one stage or other, a person needs surgical intervention with no certainty of getting cured. Blindness is the greatest curse during the advanced age. All these ailments could be prevented and cured through massage therapy.

V. Puṣṭi or Nourishment of the Tissue Elements

Tissue elements called *dhātus* in Ayurvedic parlance, are of seven categories. They are, no doubt, nourished by the intake of appropriate food. But if the enzymes which are responsible for digestion and metabolism are affected, then, in spite of appropriate food and drinks, a person does not get good health and his tissues remain undernourished. During the process of metabolism, some waste products come out because of enzymatic reaction and these are required to be eliminated from the body. At times, because of bad circulation and improper action of the nerves, these waste products continue to remain adhered to the tissues and hamper further nourishment of their cells. These waste products get eliminated from the body in the form of sweat, urine, stool, etc., through massage. Therefore, for the prevention of malnourishment and cure of already malnourished persons, massage therapy plays an important role.

IV. Āyuṣ or Longevity

The normal span of life of an individual varies from region to region depending upon the geographic, climatic, dietatic and cultural variations. While death cannot be averted, it is necessary that the person should live a full span of life and should not succumb to an untimely death. If the tissue elements and the vital organs of the body continue to function properly, then, obviously, the span of life could be prolonged and a person with a prolonged span of life and with his accumulated experience will be an asset to the society. The function of these vital organs and tissues could be improved and life span could be promoted through massage therapy.

VII. Svapna or Sleep

Man has become a machine. He continues to work constantly without giving sufficient rest to his body and mind. If an adult could get natural and deep sleep during at least 6 hours a day, then his body will be recouped for work for the next day. Because of artificial way of living, speaking and thinking, the so-called civilised person does not sleep well. He gets his sleep induced artificially by taking sleeping pills, which produce adverse effects, both on the body and the mind of the person in the long run. Apart from mental factors, there are several physical factors, which cause sleeplessness. Excessive intake of caffine in the form of tea or coffee, excessive intake of nicotine in the form of cigarette and chewing tobacco, excessive indulgence in sex and irregularity in diet, in addition to fear, worry, anxiety and mental tension give rise to sleeplessness. In order to overcome sleeplessness, and other related mental ailments massage therapy is very useful.

VIII. Dārḍhya or Sturdiness

An individual during his natural and normal course of living is exposed to several stresses and strains of life. If the body is not capable of standing firmly to these stresses and strains, then he becomes a victim of several ailments. Massage provides a passive form of exercise even for those who cannot perform active physical exercise because of debility and oldage. Even for a normal healthy person, massage provides sturdiness of the body, which keeps him healthy and happy.

Metaphoric Illustrations

The benefit of massage is described in Ayurveda in the way of different metaphoric illustrations. A leather bag gets worn out quickly if used regularly, but if it is greased in time, then it will last longer. The axle of a wheel in vehicle gets quickly worn out unless it is timely and appropriately greased. The body is compared to a tree. If the root of the tree is given water regularly, then it lives for a long time. Similarly, on the above analogy, if the body of an individual is oleated properly through massage, then he lives for a long time without any decay of disease.

Caraka (*Caraka Saṃhitā*; *Siddhasthāna* : 6 : 11-13) has described specific utility of the Oleation Therapy as follows:–

If a pot is smeared with oily substance, then water etc. in the pot, could come out very easily. Similarly, if the body is oleated, then the three disease causing factors, namely, (i) *vāyu*, (ii) *pitta*, and (iii) *kapha*, can come out of the body without much of difficulty. This is stated with reference to aggravated *vāyu, pitta* and *kapha*, which are responsible for the causation of all the diseases in the individual.

If a piece of wet-wood is ignited, then the water contents of it will exude. Similarly if fomentation therapy is applied over an oleated body, then all the waste products in the body could be easily taken out.

Massage should be Done Regularly

As a person takes food daily, so also he should resort to massage every day if he wants to keep himself healthy. To a normal healthy person, massage should be given before he takes bath, so that the excess of oil used for massage could be washed off very easily. Because of the heat produced during the process of massage, he should wait for atleast one hour before he goes for the bath. Massage is very useful before performing physical exercise. But, to those who cannot do it and for those who practise Yoga or Yogic exercises, massage can be given even after these exercises.

Time of Oil Massage

Massage should be performed only when the patient has digested the food taken during the earlier meal-time and when he is hungry and thirsty, (*Aṣṭāṅga saṅgraha*). The oil to be used for massage should be cold during summer season and it should be made warm during winter season. Mustard oil, oil cooked by adding aromatic drugs and flowers and oil cooked by adding medicinal plants can be used for massage in all seasons.

Massage and Physical Exercises

Massage can be applied over the body before as well as after physical exercise. By massage, blood circulation in the body improves and removes stiffness of various joints of the body as a result of which movement of the organs during the exercise is facilitated. If massage is applied after the exercise, then it helps in the removal of metabolic waste products from the body through the gastro-intestinal tract.

Auspicious Days

Information on auspicious and inauspicious days for massage therapy is provided in texts on Astrology. Massage on Mondays, Wednesdays and Saturdays is very auspicious inasmuch as it bestows auspiciousness and wealth and promotes longevity.

On Sundays, massage should be done by cooking oil with *dūrvā* (*Cynodon dactylon*) and on Tuesdays, oil for massage should be cooked by adding aromatic flowers.

Inauspicious Days

Massage should not be done on the 3rd, 6th, 8th, 10th, 11th, 13th and 14th day of a lunar fortnight.

On the 3rd day, massage causes unhappiness.
On the 6th day, massage causes reduction in the span of life.
On the 8th day, massage anihilates religious virtues.
On the 10th day, massage leads to son's death.
On the 11th day, massage destroys complexion.
On the 13th day, massage destroys wealth.
On the 14th day, massage gives rise to several obstinate diseases.

Therefore, on the above mentioned days of the lunar fortnight, one should avoid massage.

In addition to the above days of the fortnight, one should avoid massage on religious festival days, on the days of *śrāddha* (when offerings are made to dead ancestors) and during the constellations of *Śrāvaṇā, Ārdrā, Jyeṣṭhā, Uttarā phālgunā* and on *saṅkrānti* days (when the sun moves from one zordiac sign to the other). This prohibition does not apply to small infants and old persons.

Massage in Prohibited Days

The above mentioned prohibitions apply to massage with sesame oil. But even during prohibited days massage can be done with the following:

(1) Mustard oil
(2) Oil cooked with aromatic flowers
(3) Oil cooked by adding different medicinal plants and their products.

Signs and Symptoms of Appropriate Oleation Tnerapy

Sneha is the term used in Ayurveda to indicate all types of fatty substances like oil, ghee, etc. In fact, this is derived from the root *snih*, which means "to be adhessive", "to be attached to" or "to be fond of" or to "feel affection for". If the body is properly oleated either through internal use of ghee, etc., or through massage, then there will be smoothness, softness and stickiness of the body. It alleviates *vāyu* and helps in the detachment of the waste products. It is an excellent therapy for the promotion of digestion and metabolism. If a person is accustomed to taking oil, ghee, etc., regularly, then the intake of even very heavy food does not give rise to any ailment.

Contra-Indications

Massage should not be given to:

1. A patient suffering from fever (in its first stage) and indigestion. If such a person is given massage, then his disease becomes incurable.
2. A person who has been administered purgation, emetic and enema therapies. If such a person is given massage, then his power of digestion gets suppressed.
3. A person suffering from diseases caused by over-nourishment. By massage, his disease gets further aggravated.

Massage even though indicated to be performed regularly every day, in certain circumstances, this is prohibited. It should not be performed during the first stage of the fever, if there is indigestion and if there is *āma* (uncooked material) during the process of digestion and metabolism. If a person is suffering from diseases as a result of aggravation of *kapha*, then also massage is prohibited, because *kapha* (phlegm) and *āma* are very closely related. It is specially prohibited for a person suffering from obesity. If, however, such a person suffers from any disease in which massage is strongly indicated and even for the cure of obesity, massage oil, etc., can be prepared by a special method and used for massage.

Modes of Administering Massage Therapy

Massage therapy can be administered to a person in two different ways as follows:

(1) It can be administered regularly to a person for the prevention of several diseases and for the maintenance as well as promotion of positive health. Generally, it is done before taking bath. By taking bath after massage, excess of oil from the skin is removed and whatever oil or fat remains over the skin is sufficient to produce the expected effects.
(2) It can also be done as a special therapy for a limited period as will be described later. This type of special massage therapy is generally administered for:

   (a) the purpose of rejuvenating the body to prevent and arrest the ageing process; and
   (b) curing several obstinate and otherwise incurable diseases.

Apart from the above mentioned purposes, massage therapy along with fomentation is also given before administering several categories of elimination therapies like emesis (*vamana*), purgation (*virecana*), two types of medicated enema (*nirūha* and *anuvāsana*) and inhalation (*nasya*) as well as blood-letting (*rakta mokṣaṇa*) therapies. Taken together, these elimination therapies in ayurvedic parlance are called *Pañca karma* or five specialised therapies. According to Caraka, the following five are included in *Pañca karma*:

(1) *Vamana* (Emetic therapy);
(2) *Virecana* (Purgation therapy);

(3) *Nirūha* (A type of medicated enema containing mostly decoctions of plants, etc.);
(4) *Anuvāsana* (A type of medicated enema containing mostly oil, etc.); and
(5) *Nasya* (Inhalation therapy).

Suśruta has mentioned *rakta mokṣaṇa* or blood-letting therapy in the place of *nasya* or inhalation therapy discribed above. *Vāgbhaṭa* has however, described both *nasya* and *rakta mokṣaṇa* under this category of specialised elimination therapies.

Massage over the Whole or Parts of the Body

Regular massage should be performed over the whole body including head for the prevention of diseases, promotion of positive health, rejuvenation of the individual and cure of diseases. But massage in specific parts of the body has some special effects. Massage at times is performed over these specific parts only. These parts are as follows:

(1) Head massage (*Śiro'bhyaṅga*)
(2) Gentle massage after pouring oil into the ears (*Karṇa pūraṇa*)
(3) Massage over the soles of the feet (*Pādābhyaṅga*).

Their specific attributes are described hereafter.

4

HEAD MASSAGE (SIRO'BHYAṄGA)

In addition to massage all over the body, in certain circumstances, massage over only particular part of the body is found to be useful. Head is the most important organ of the body because all the senses and sense organs like eyes, nose, ears, tongue and skin are located in it. Therefore, massage over the head provides nourishment to ali these senses and promotes their normal and natural functions. Head massage is specially useful for the following:

1. It prevents and cures headache.
2. It prevents and cures hair-fall.
3. It prevents and cures premature greying of hair.
4. It prevents and cures baldness.
5. It makes the hair-root very strong.
6. It makes the hair long, soft and glossy.
7. It prevents and cures refraction errors of the eyes.
8. It promotes complexion of the face.
9. It endows a person with sound sleep.

Apart from massage, the oil also can be applied over the head for the above mentioned benefits in the form of *śirobasti*, which will be described later.

5

FILLING THE EARS WITH OIL (KARṆA PŪRAṆA)

By pouring oil into the ears, several diseases specific to this sense organ like earache, deafness, tinitus and several diseases of the nearby organs like headache, lock-jaw, torticolis and giddiness are cured. This also corrects diseases of the teeth and the gums.

Ears and eyes are very closely related to the soles of the feet. Pouring oil into the ears produces coldness and removes burning sensation in the feet.

Pouring of medicated oil into the ears should be performed before meals during the day time.

6

MASSAGE OVER THE SOLES OF THE FEET (PĀDĀBHYAṄGA)

Before going to bed, it is very useful to have a massage over the soles of feet. It prevents and cures dryness, numbness, roughness, fatigue, and lack of sensation and cracking in the soles of feet. It promotes strength for walking and running, and gives sturdiness to the limbs. Soles of the feet are very closely connected with eyes and ears. Therefore, massage over the soles of the feet promotes eye-sight and proper functioning of the auditory organs of the ears. It also cures sciatica, cramps and contraction of the ligaments, vessels and muscles of the lower limbs.

Above all, massage helps a person to have sound sleep at night.

Vāgbhaṭa (*Aṣṭāṅga-hṛdaya: Uttara tantra*: 15: 66-67) has furnished a beautiful description of the effect of massage over the soles of the feet. According to him, there are four important nerves in the soles of the feet, which are connected with the head. Because of heat, friction and excessive pressure on the soles of the feet, these nerves get afflicted as a result of which, eye-sight of a person gets reduced. If at the root of these nerves i.e. in the soles of the feet, massage is done regularly, then the person never suffers from any eye disease.

Time Taken to Permeate Through Different Tissues

According to ayurveda, oil, etc., used for massage do not have their actions confined to the skin alone. Oil, etc., and the drugs with which these are boiled permeate through the skin and reach different tissue elements of the body. The medicated oil used for massage remain in the skin for 300 seconds (*mātrās*) and then gradually and consecutively permeates through different tissue elements like *rakta* (blood), *māṃsa* (muscle tissue), *medas* (fat tissue), *asthi* (bone tissue) and *majjā* (bone marrow). The medicated oil takes about 100 seconds (*mātrās*) each, to pervade and permeate through these different categories of tissue elements.

Other Methods of Massage

Apart from massage with oil, ghee and different other types of fat, this therapy can be administered with the pastes and powders of medicinal plants, etc. in different ways.

7

UDVARTANA OR UNCTION

If the paste of drugs is applied over the body, allowed to dry up slightly and then gently rubbed to remove this paste, then this type of therapy is called *udvartana* or unction.

Benefits of Udvartana

The person using *udvartana* or unction therapy gets endowed with the following benefits:

1. It removes foul smell from the body.
2. It cures heaviness, drowsiness, itching, diseases caused by waste products, anorexia, excessive sweating and disfiguration of the skin.
3. It alleviates *vāyu*.
4. It helps in the melting of *kapha* and fat.
5. It produces stability of the limbs.
6. It promotes skin health.
7. It opens up the orifices of the channels of circulation.
8. It promotes the enzymes responsible for the metabolic processes in the skin as a result of which the skin remains healthy.
9. It specially promotes the complexion of females and removes unwanted hair from their face and body.

Recipe for Udvartana

The recipe for unction should have the following ingredients:

1. *Kuṣṭha*	(root)	*(Saussurrea lappa)*
2. *Mustā*	(root)	*(Cyperus rotundus)*

3. *Granthi parṇī*	(root)	*(Angelica glauca)*
4. *Haridrā*	(rhizome)	*(Curcuma longa)*
5. *Dāru haridrā*	(root or stem)	*(Berberis aristata)*
6. *Bālā* or *hrībera*	(root)	*(Coleus vettiveroides)*
7. *Jaṭāmāṃsī*	(root)	*(Nardostachys jatamansi)*
8. *Vājigandhā*	(root)	*(Withania somnifera)*
9. *Puṣkara mūla*	(root)	*(Inula racemosa)*
10. *Nimba*	(leaf)	*(Azadirachta indica)*
11. *Āragvadha*	(leaf)	*(Cassia fistula)*
12. *Tulasī*	(leaf)	*(Ocimum sanctum)*
13. *Arjuna*	(leaf)	*(Terminalia arjuna)*
14. *Elā*	(seed)	*(Amomum subulatum)*
15. *Ajājī*	(seed)	*(Nigella sativa)*
16. *Sarṣapa*	(seed)	*(Brassica compestris)*
17. *Tila*	(seed)	*(Sesamum indicum)*
18. *Dhānyaka*	(seed)	*(Coriandrum sativum)*
19. *Bākucī*	(seed)	*(Psoralea corylifolia)*
20. *Cakramarda*	(seed)	*(Cassia tora)*
21. *Lavaṅga*	(flower)	*(Syzygium aromaticum)*
22. *Padmaka*	(bark)	*(Prunus cerasoides)*
23. *Lodhra*	(bark)	*(Symplocos racemosa)*
24. *Candana*	(heart-wood)	*(Santalum album)*
25. *Devadāru*	(heart-wood)	*(Cedrus deodara)*
26. *Agaru*	(heart-wood)	*(Aquilaria agallocha)*
27. *Sarala*	(heart-wood)	*(Pinus roxburghii)*
28. *Nāgakesara*	(flower)	*(Mesua ferrea)*
29. *Punnāga*	(flower)	*(Calophyllum inophyllum)*
30. *Karkandhu*	(flower)	*(Zizyphus nummularia)*
31. *Nimba*	(flower)	*(Azadirachta indica)*
32. *Guggulu*	(gum-resin)	*(Commiphora mukul)*
33. *Saindhava*		*(rock-salt)*
34. *Bola*	(resin)	*(Commiphora myrrha)*
35. *Sarjarasa*	(resin)	*(Vateria indica)*

The above mentioned ingredients should be dried in shade. Except for the gums and salt, all the other items should first be made to power. Thereafter, gums and salt should be added to this. The recipe should then be triturated by adding milk or water. Colouring material may also be added to them. This paste should be used for unction.

8

UDGHARṢAṆA OR RUBBING THE BODY WITH POWDERS

Apart from the paste described above, medicinal plants, etc., can also be used for rubbing (massage) over the body which is called *udgharṣaṇa* (powder-rubbing). This type of massage has the following benefits:

1. It cures itching, urticaria and diseases caused by *vāyu*;
2. It produces stability and lightness in the body;
3. Rubbing the skin after sprinkling water gives rise of foam. Thus, rubbing with soapnut powder has the above-mentioned properties. In additions, it promotes the activities of the enzymes in the skin and it helps in removing dirt from the openings of sweat glands.

9

DIFFERENT TYPES OF FAT USED IN MASSAGE THERAPY

For massage therapy fat should be collected from the following different sources:

1. *Taila* or oil collected from seeds and different other parts of the plant.
2. *Ghṛta* or ghee collected from milk (or curd i.e. yoghurt) of different types of animals including human-milk. Butter of these animals is also used for massage.
3. *Vasā* or fat collected by boiling the muscle tissue of animal. The fat of animals like pig is also used for massage.
4. *Majjā* or bone-marrow (both white and red varieties) are also used for massage

Properties of Different Types of Fat

For *snehana* or oleation therapy including massage, four types of fats, viz., ghee, oil, fat and bone-marrow are generally used. Their specific attributes are as follows:

I. Ghee (Ghṛta)

It has the following properties:

1. It alleviates *pitta* and *vāyu* but does not cause aggravation of *kapha*.
2. It promotes *rasa* (chyle), semen and *ojas* (essence of all the tissue elements).
3. It alleviates burning sensation.
4. It produces softness of the body.

5. It promotes good voice and complexion.
6. It promotes strength and the power of digestion as well as metabolism.
7. Because of its unctuosness, it alleviates *vāyu* and because of its cooling property, it alleviates *pitta*. When it is cooked with *kapha*-alleviating drugs, it also alleviates *kapha*.
8. It has the specific feature of the *yogavāhin* (carrying the properties of other drugs with which it is cooked). It is one of the best among the fats.

II. Oil (Taila)

It has the following properties:

1. It alleviates *vāyu* but does not aggravate *kapha*.
2. It promotes strength, skin-health and stability of the body.
3. It cleanses the genito-urinary tract specially that of the females.

III. Muscle Fat (Vasā)

It has the following properties:

1. It heals wounds and broken bones.
2. It is useful in prolapse of uterus.
3. It cures headache and earache.
4. It promotes vision.
5. It is very useful for persons accustomed to strenuous physical exercise.

IV. Bone Marrow (Majjā)

It has the followiing properties:

1. It promotes strength, semen and *rasa* (chyle and plasma).
2. It increases the quality of *kapha*, *medas* (fat) and bone-marrow.
3. It specially promotes the strength of bones.

Comparison of Properties

Muscle fat (*vasā*) is better than marrow (*majjā*), oil is better than muscle fat, and ghee is better than oil in promoting oleation of the body. For the purpose of massage, however, oil (including medicated oil) is the best. For internal use, ghee is undoubtedly the best.

Oil of Oil Seeds

Among the different types of oil collected from oil seeds, sesame oil is the best. It can be used for massage alone or after being cooked by adding different drugs.

Properties of Sesame Oil

Apart from oleation, oil collected from different types of oil-seeds or different other parts of medicinal plants has some specific properties. In massage therapy, both for therapeutic purpose and for the purpose of rejuvenation, generally sesame or til oil is used. Its general properties are given below:

> Sesame oil is predominantly sweet in taste. It is also astringent in its subsidiary taste. It also has the property to penetrate through the subtle channels of the body. It is hot in potency. It is *vyavāyin* i.e. it undergoes metabolic transformation after it has pervaded all over the body. It, at times, aggravates *pitta* but does not aggravate *kapha*. It is the best among the alleviators of *vāyu*. It promotes strength, skin health, intelligence and the power of digestion. In combination with other drugs, sesame oil helps in the cure of all diseases.
>
> Apart from sesame oil, and oil collected from other plants, water, milk, yoghurt (curd), butter-milk, butter and animal fat are also used in massage therapy. Their properties and those of other ingredients used in massage, as described in Madanapāla's *Nighaṇṭu* are furnished at *Appendix I*.

Different Types of Oil used for Different Specific Purposes

Oil collected from different seeds and other parts of plants can be used both externally (for massage) and internally. These oils, useful for different therapeutic purposes, are described below.

I. Laxative

For laxative effects, oils collected from the following plants (seeds) are useful:

1. *Tilvaka (Symplocos racemosa)*
2. *Eraṇḍa (Ricinus communis)*
3. *Kośāmra (Schleichera oleosa)*
4. *Dantī (Baliospermum montanum)*
5. *Dravantī (Croton tiglium)*
6. *Saptalā (Acacia concinna)*
7. *Śaṅkhinī (Calonyction muricatum)*
8. *Palāśa (Butea monosperma)*
9. *Meṣaśṛṅgī (Pistacia integerrima)*
10. *Indrāyaṇa (Citrullus colocynthis)*
11. *Kampillaka (Mallotus philippinensis)*
12. *Āragvadha (Cassia fistula)*
13. *Nilinī (Indigofera tinctoria)*

II. Emetic

For emesis, oils collected from the following plants (seeds) are useful:

1. *Devadālī (Luffa echinata)*
2. *Kuṭaja (Holarrhena antidysenterica)*
3. *Kośātakī (Luffa acutangula)*
4. *Ikṣvāku* or *Kaṭutumbī (Lagenaria siceraria)*
5. *Dhāmārgava* or *Mahākośātakī (Luffa cylindrica)*
6. *Madanaphala (Randia dumetorum)*

III. Elimination of Waste Products from Head

For elimination of *doṣas* from the head (*śiro virecana*), oils collected from the following plants (seeds) are useful:

1. *Viḍaṅga (Embelia ribes)*
2. *Apāmārga (Achyranthes aspera)*
3. *Śobhāñjana (Moringa pterygosperma)*
4. *Sūryavallī (Gynandropis gynandra)*

5. *Pīlu (Salvadora persica)*
6. *Sarṣapa (Brassica campestris)*
7. *Jyotiṣmatī (Celastrus paniculatus)*

IV. Ulcer-healing

For the healing of ulcers, oil collected from the following plants (seeds) is useful:

1. *Karañja (Pongamia pinnata)*
2. *Latākarañja (Caesalpinia crista)*
3. *Āragvadha (Cassia fistula)*
4. *Mātuluṅga (Citrus medica)*
5. *Iṅgudī (Balanites agyptica)*
6. *Kirāta tikta (Swertia chirata)*

V. Skin Diseases

For the treatment of *kuṣṭha* (obstinate skin diseases including leprosy), oil collected from the following plants (seeds) is useful:

1. *Tuvaraka (Hydṇocarpus wightiana)*
2. *Kapittha (Feronia limonia)*
3. *Kampillaka (Mallotus philippinensis)*
4. *Bhallātaka (Semecarpus anacardium)*
5. *Paṭola (Trichosanthes cucumerina)*

VI. Urinary Disorders

For the treatment of *mūtrasaṅga* (anuria), oil collected from the following plants (seeds) is useful:

1. *Trapusa (Cucumis sativus)*
2. *Karkaṭī* or *ervāruka (Cucumis utilissimus)*
3. *Kuṣmāṇḍa (Cucurbita pepo)*
4. *Tumbī (Lagenaria siceraria)*
5. *Karkāru (Cucurbita maxima)*

VII. Calculus in Urinary Tract

For the treatment of stone in the urinary tract, the oil collected from the following plants is useful:

1. *Brāhmī* or *Kapotavaṅkā or suvrcalā (Bacopa monnieri)*
2. *Bākuci (Psoralea corylifolia)*
3. *Harītakī (Terminalia chebula)*

VIII. Obstinate Urinary Disorders

For the treatment of *prameha* (obstinate urinary disorders including diabetes), oil collected from the following plants (seeds) is useful:

1. *Sarṣapa (Brassica compestris)*
2. *Atasī (Linum usitatissimum)*
3. *Nimba (Azadirachta indica)*
4. *Mādhavī (Hiptage benghalensis)*
5. *Mañjiṣṭhā (Rubia cordifolia)*
6. *Kaṭutumbī (Lagenaria siceraria)*
7. *Jyotiṣmatī (Celastrus paniculatus)*

IX. Nervous Disorders

For the treatment of ailments caused by *vāyu* associated with vitiated *pitta*, oil from the following plants (seeds) is useful:

1. *Tāla (Borassus flabellifer)*
2. *Nārikela (Cocus nucifera)*
3. *Panasa (Artocarpus heterophyllus)*
4. *Moca (Salmalia malabarica)*
5. *Priyāla (Buchanania lanzan)*
6. *Bilva (Aegle marmelos)*
7. *Madhūka (Madhuca indica)*
8. *Śleṣmāntaka (Cordia myxa)*
9. *Āmrātaka (Spondias pinnata)*

X. Leucoderma

For the treatment of white patches in the skin (to make the skin black by pigmentation), oil collected from the following plants (seeds) is useful:

1. *Bibhītaka (Terminalia belerica)*
2. *Bhallātaka (Semecarpus anacardium)*
3. *Madanaphala (Randia dumetorum)*

XI. Hyper-pigmentation

For correcting excessive pigmentation of the skin, oil collected from the following plants is useful:

1. *Iṅgudī (Balanites agyptiaca)*
2. *Priyaṅgu (Callicarpa macrophylla)*
3. *Śyonāka (Oroxylum indicum)*

XII. Minor Skin Disorders

For the treatment of minor skin diseases like ringworm, the oil of the following plants (seeds) is useful:

1. *Sarala (Pinus roxburghii)*
2. *Pītadāru (Berberis aristata)*
3. *Śiṃśapā (Dalbergia sissoo)*
4. *Aguru (Aquilaria agallocha)*

10

SPECIAL MASSAGE THERAPIES

In Ayurveda, several therapies have been prescribed in which massage and fomentation are given together. These therapies are even now prevalent and popularly administered in South India particularly in Kerala. Generally, this type of therapy is used by healthy persons for the purpose of rejuvenation. In addition, these are also administered to different types of patients for curing of their diseases.

11

PIṆḌASVEDA OR NAVARAKIZHI

It is one of the most popular therapies used for the purpose of rejuvenation of the body. It is a process by which, the whole body or a part of it is made to perspire by the application of certain medicinal puddings followed by massage. The commonly followed method is given below.

Preparation of Decoction and Pudding

The root of the plant called *balā (Sida rhombifolia)* is popularly used for this therapy. About 500 gms. of the root of this plant is used for this purpose. After being washed pr' perly, cut into chips and crushed well, these roots are put into 8 liters of water approximately. This is then boiled till the water evaporates and ¼th of it remains. This decoction is then strained through a strainer or linen. The decoction, now remains is approximately 2 litres in quantity. Half of this dedoction i.e. approximately 1 litre is added with 1 litre of cow's milk and the other 1 litre of decoction is kept for use at a later stage. To the above mentioned decoction and the milk (1 litre each), about 500 gms, of rice (dehusked paddy) is added and cooked till it becomes semi-solid like a pudding. Generally, this pudding is called *pāyasam* (milk and rice preparation). A type of paddy called *ṣaṣṭika*, *nīvāra* or *navara* (Bot. *Oryza picta*) is generally used for this preparation. This *navara* paddy is again of two types – one is of white colour and the other is blackish white. It is the former which is very useful for this therapy. In case of its non-availability, even though it is very cheap, ordinary type of rice may also used by the physician for the preparation of this pudding or milk product *(pāyasam)*. It is important also that the rice should be absolutely free from any husk. In certain parts of India, paddy as a whole is, first of all, boiled dried and then it is dehusked. But, for this recipe, rice collected from raw and un boiled (paddy) is to be used. It is not necessary to wash this rice with water before boiling. After dehusking the paddy, the rice should be cleaned. After removing the parts of the husk, stone and other foreign material, it should be added to the mixture of the decoction and the milk for cooking. It is desirable to crush the rice-grains into small pieces before boiling.

Cloth-Pieces

Eight pieces of new clean cloth, which are neither too thick nor too rough, but moderately smooth and tough to withstand the strain of the process that will follow, should be taken. Each piece should be 40 cm. in length and breadth and its edges should be well stitched so that threads do not come out of its loose ends during the process of application of the therapy (Fig. 1).

Preparation of Boluses

Pudding prepared according to the process described above should be divided into eight equal parts and kept in these eight pieces of cloth. The edges of these cloth pieces should be gathered together and tied with the help of a rope, each of them separately, to form eight boluses (bundles). The ends of cloth pieces should be left free i.e. untied to facilitate holding them easily with hand by the masseure during massage. Generally, physicians prefer to perform some religious rituals just at the beginning of the therapy. Before massage with the help of these bundles of pudding, the body of the patient should be properly prepared (Fig. 2).

Application of Oil

The body of the patient should be anointed with medicated oil. The oil to be applied over the head should be slightly different from the oil to be applied over the body. The oil of the head should not be very greasy, whereas the one for the body is normally very greasy. Different types of medicated oils are used depending upon the purpose for which the therapy is administered. For healthy persons and for the purpose of rejuvenation, different types of oil are used. For instance, if the patient is suffering from any disease, the medicated oil has to be prepared by boiling with such drugs as would cure that disease. The type of medicated oil to be used in this therapy

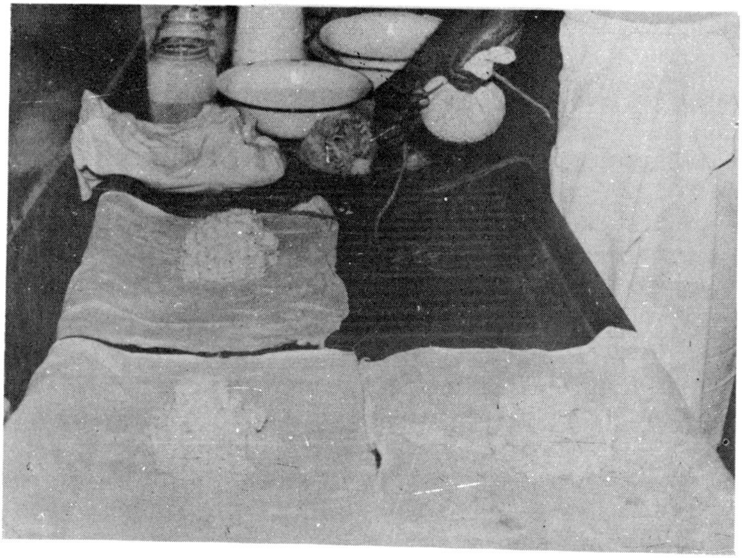

FIG. 1: *Piṇḍa* or Medicated Rice bolus being tied with a string

FIG. 2: Four *Piṇḍas* or Medicated rice boluses being kept ready before massage

has to be selected by the physician earlier after proper examination of the patient.

Need for Oil-Massage

Without applying this oil, *piṇḍa-sveda* should not be applied to the patient. Earlier massage with the oil helps in maintaining uniformity of the heat to be applied during the therapy through these pudding bundles. The oil also protects the skin from sudden evaporation and perspiration. If the patient is suddenly exposed to cold immediately after the application of the hot pudding and massage, then he is likely to suffer from several respiratory diseases.

Protection of Eyes

The oil from the head should not trickle down to the face and eyes of the patient, as this may give rise to irritation to the eyes and a sense of discomfort to the patient. Therefore, a piece of cloth should be tied round the head at the level of the eye-brows to prevent the flow of oil from the head to the eyes.

Massage Table

For the administration of this therapy, a special type of table is used. For the preparation of this table, heart-wood of neem, *khadira (Acacia catechu), asana (Pterocarpus marsupium), arjuna (Terminalia arjuna)* or mango is used. Generally, the table is prepared (carved) out of a single piece of wood and there should not be any joint at the base of the table.

Traditionally, the massage is given by the masseures while sitting (squatting) on the floor. Therefore, the table for this purpose is not very high. (Fig.3) But if the masseures prefer, as at present, to give massage while in standing position, then the table should have a pedestal to stand on it and the height of this stand should be as per the requirement. An adjustable stand can be fixed below the table so that masseures of different height can use it conveniently. The masseures should however, of the similar height to enable them to exercise uniform pressure on the patient during the process of the massage.

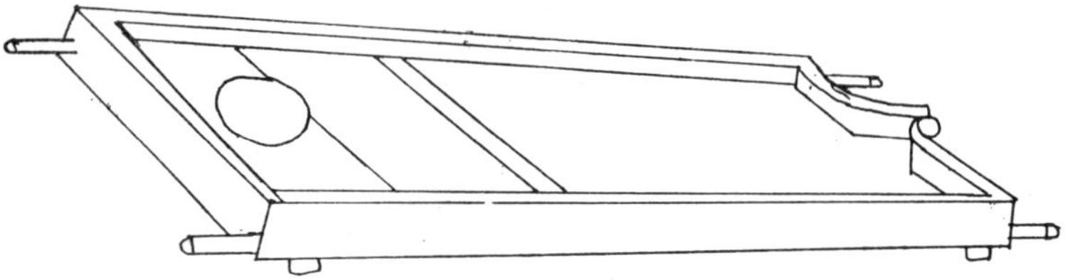

FIG. 3: Traditional Massage Table without Pedestal

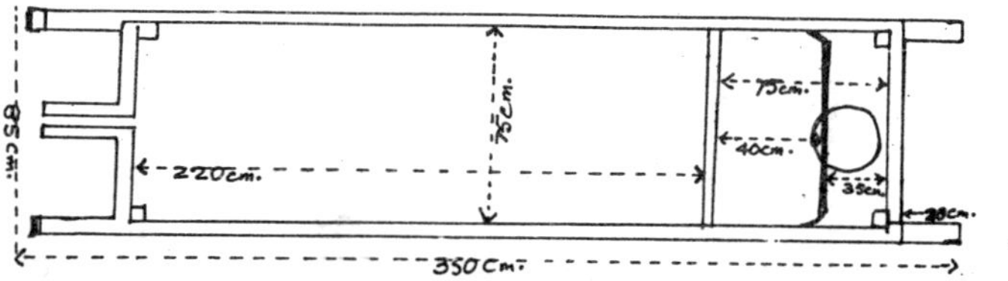

FIG. 4: Measurements of the Traditional Massage Table

Generally, the piece of wood to be selected for the purpose of preparing this table should be 350 cm. long, 85 cm. broad and 25 cm. thick. From both ends of the piece of wood, 20 cm. should be cut out at the centre in such a manner so as to provide four rounded handles at the four corners (at the bottom). Each handle should be 20 cm. long and 4 cm. in diameter for the convenience of holding it while changing its position. Leaving a margin of 5 cm. all around, the remaining surface of the table should be carved (scooped) out so that the floor of the basin should be 3 cm. deep every where. Thereafter, the table is divided into two compartments – one for keeping the head which should be 75 cm. long and the other for resting the body which should be 220 cm. long. In between these two compartments, there should be an elevated ridge of about 5 cm. Over this ridge the neck of the patient should be rest during the process of massage (vide Fig. 4).

The compartment for head is again divided into two distinct segments – one at the proximal end being 40 cm. long and the other at the distal end being 35 cm. long. The former part should slope towards the distal side while the latter should have normal level. For supporting the head, a circular pit of 20 cm. in diameter should be scooped out and it should have a slope towards the centre. There should be a small hole at the centre of this circular pit through which the excess oil from the head could be conveniently drained out of the platform.

In the second compartment meant for resting the body, two small holes should be made at the two distal ends in the corner to let out the excess oil from the table. In addition, drainage facility should be provided at the center of the lower border. Traditionally, only the central drainage is provided and holes at the corners are avoided.

Bowls should be kept below these holes to receive the drained oil and the oil should not be allowed to spill over the floor. Then the chambers for the head and the body should be made smooth and the elevated borders should be rounded up so that the patient could comfortably lie over it during the process of the therapy. (Fig.5)

This table should then be fixed over an appropriate pedestal or frame having four legs. It should be ensured that the table does not move or make noise during the massage because of loose screws.

The patient should first of all be made to sit over this table before the commencement of the therapy. Half the decoction of *balā (Sida rhombifolia)*, which was prepared earlier and kept separately, should now be kept in a pan, added with equal quantity of cow's milk and placed over an oven or stove having mild fire. The pudding-bundles should then be placed in the pan and allowed to become warm. These pudding-bundles during the process of massage, loose heat and become gradually cold.

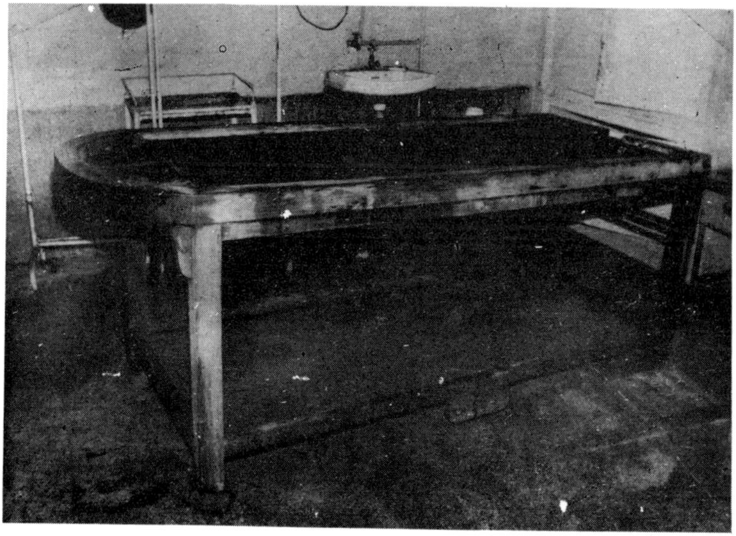

FIG. 5: Modern Massage table with a Pedestal

In this therapy, it is essential that all through the process, a uniform temprature should be maintained, and therefore, the warmth of these pudding-bundles should be continuously uniform. For this purpose, these pudding-bundles should be repeatedly immersed in the above mentioned boiling decoction and milk.

The oven which is used for boiling the decoction should be free from smoke and excess of heat to prevent irritation and a feeling of displeasure by the patient and the masseurs.

The room should be well-ventilated and well-lighted taking care to see that the patient is not exposed to draughts, dust or direct sun-rays, To ensure this, the doors, windows of the room should be provided with curtains made of thin fabrics.

Masseurs

This therapy involves giving general massage to the patient with the help of pudding-bundles prepared earlier. Four masseurs are required to apply this therapy. Apart from the physician, who will be supervising the process, there should be another attendant who will help in collecting the cold bundles from the masseurs and supplying the warm ones to them from the boiling decoction. The masseurs should be quiet (not talkative) and fully attentive to their duty. By their behaviour, they should not cause annoyance or displeasure to the patient. If a female patient has to be given this therapy, then it is better to employ female masseurs and attendants. In case of their non-availability, old and experienced male masseurs can also be employed. But it is essential that these masseurs and attendents should maintain absolute decorum during the process of the therapy. The room should be commodious for free movement of the attendants and the supervising physician. It should be secluded and away from the residential areas to maintain privacy of the patient.

The patient will have to remove his clothes and should wear only a loin cloth or under-wear. In the beginning, he is to be in a sitting posture. Four of these eight pudding-bundles are to be taken by the four masseurs. Earlier these bundles were kept in the mixture of milk and decoction and made tolerably warm. Thereafter, these bundles are to be held outside for four or five minutes to reduce excessive heat and to make them comfortably warm for the massage. Each masseur should take one of these bundles which should be held by the right hand by its tuft and then the base of the pudding-bundle is to be placed over the back of the left hand to check the heat.

Thereafter, the masseurs should start giving massage to the patient. The direction of the massage should be always from upwards to downwards beginning from the neck area. Two of these masseurs remain in the right side of the patient and the remaining two on the left side. Two of them standing near the head should give massage from the neck to the hip and the other two standing near the thighs should give massage from the hip to the sole of the foot. On both the sides, massage should be given simultaneously and at the same time. Every care should be taken to ensure uniformity of temperature and pressure on all parts of the body.

When the first four pudding-bundles are in use, the other four are to be kept in the mixture of decoction and milk placed over the fire. When the earlier ones cool down, they are placed in the pan and the warm ones are taken out of it for use. The massage should be conducted without any appreciable interruption or break. Therefore, replacing the cold pudding-bundles with the hot ones should be as quick as possible.

Position of Body

The patient should first be on the massage table in the (i) sitting posture. After massage for sometime, he is to be made to lie on his (2) back and the massage should be continued in this position. Thereafter, he is to be made to lie on (3) the right side, again on his (4) back, and then on the (5) left side, once again on his (6) back and finally he should revert back to the (7) erect sitting posture. Massage is done in all these seven various postures. In each of these postures, massage should be done for 15 minutes approximately. Thus, the whole process may take one hour and 45 minutes to two hours. The time of the therapy can, however, be increased or decreased depending upon the general condition and strength of the patient and the disease he is sufering from. The physician has to assess the exact requirements of the patient. (Fig. 6 to 9)

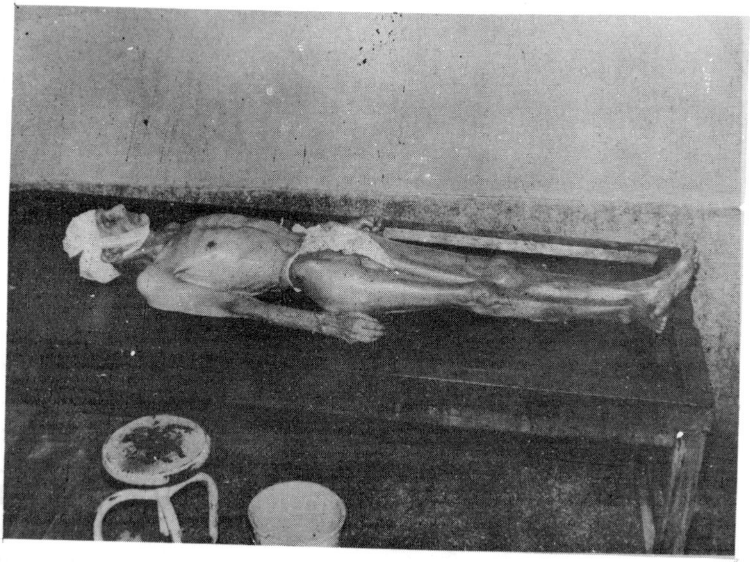

FIG. 6: The patient in lying position. The head is traditionally covered with the paste of *āmalakī* and tied with a bandage before massage

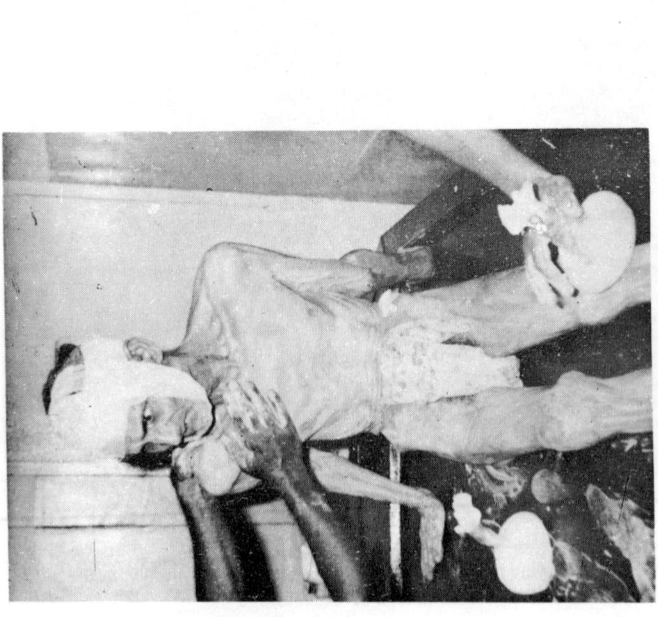

FIG. 7: The massage of chest. *Piṇḍa* is kept down. Because the patient is emaciated, to begin with, the massage is done with the paste squeezed out of the paste

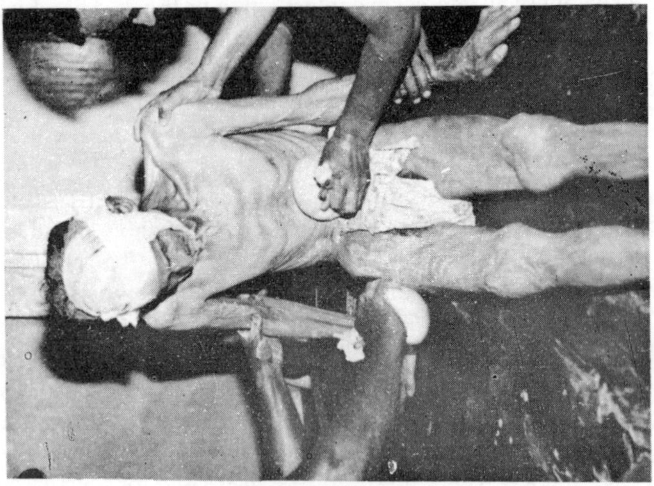

FIG. 8: Massage of the abdomen

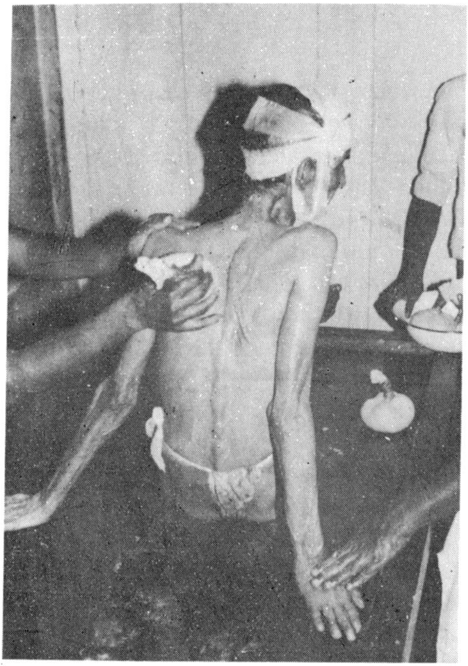

FIG 9: Massage of the back

During the process of massage, generally the mixture of decoction and milk, which is kept over the oven for boiling, gets completely used up, because the bundles of the pudding has to be frequently dipped into it. After massage, these bundles are to be opened and the remaining portion of the pudding is to be taken out. This is to be applied over the body of the patient and gently rubbed according to the procedure followed for massage. This should be done for about five minutes. Thereafter, the pudding remaining adhered to the skin of the patient should be scrapped out with the help of a thin but blunt spatula or knife. Traditionally, it is done with the help of a coconut leaf. The oil of the head is removed by gently wiping with the help of a dry towel. The scrapping of the pudding and wiping out of the oil from the head should be done gently in order to avoid production of heat by friction etc.

The head and the body, thus cleaned, are to be anointed with medicated oils. The medicated oil to be used for this purpose should be according to the necessity of the patient and it is to be specially selected by the physician. Then, the patient should be given bath.

Bath

For bathing, the water should be boiled by adding some medicinal herbs, which are to be selected by the physician. After boiling, the herbs should be filtered out and the water should be allowed to cool till it becomes luke-warm. For head, however, water should not be warm at all. The water to be used for washing the head should be of normal room temperature.

In order to remove excess oil from the body and the head, the flour of green gram or chick-pea should be rubbed. It is better if an attendant is employed for giving bath to the patient, because the patient himself may not be able to apply the above mentioned flour uniformly in all parts of his body.

After the bath, the patient should be wrapped with a cotton or woollen blanket depending upon the nature of the season and climatic conditions and should be made to take rest for about an hour. He should not be disturbed by noise or exposed to the sun, dust, storm, cold wind and smoke. It is better if the patient while lying down recites *'Om'* or *'Gāyatri Mantra'*. People of different religions can recite the holy scriptures of their respective faiths. The patient should not sleep during this time and light food can be given to him thereafter.

Course of Therapy

The course of treatment varies depending upon the strength and nature of the disease the patient is suffering from. The therapy can be applied daily or on alternate days for a period of 7 to 14 days at a stretch. The course of treatment has to be decided by the physician. Traditionally, a course of this therapy may last for 7, 9, 11 or 14 days.

For every alternate therapy, the position of the body of the patient should be changed. Masseurs are of different types and in spite of all precautions, they may be putting different types of pressure while performing massage. Changing the posture of the body alternately during alternate therapy, will eliminate this likely defect.

Some restrictions are required to be observed in respect of diet and regimens during the course of the therapy and for an equal number of days after the therapy is over details of which will be described later.

This therapy endows several benefits to a healthy person and to a patient. This causes both oleation and simultaneous fomentation of the body. It makes the body supple, removes stiffness and swelling in joints and cures diseases caused by the aggravation of *vāyu*. Once the channels of circulation are cleansed of obstructions, the blood circulation becomes better and it removes waste products from the body. It improves the complexion of the skin, increases *pitta*, promotes digestion and restores vigour. It prevents excessive sleep, but endows the person with sound sleep during the night. This therapy is very effective in curing diseases of the nervous system, chronic rheumatism, osteo-arthritis, gout, emaciation of muscles in the limbs and cures diseases caused by the vitiation of the blood. It makes the body strong and sturdy with well-developed musculature. It promotes sharpness of the vision and the functions of other sensory organs. It is very effective for persons having insomnia, high blood pressure, diabetes and obstinate skin diseases. It prevents the process of ageing, premature greying of the hair, baldness, appearance of wrinkles over the body and other ailments caused by the process of ageing.

It can be given to persons of all ages – both males and females. One should be careful in administering this therapy to persons suffering from ailments of heart. However, if proper care is taken to maintain uniformity in temperature during the process of massage, there will be no untoward effect.

12

KĀYASEKA OR PIZHICHIL

For the treatment of diseases caused by the impairment of the functioning of the nervous system, this is, perhaps, the best therapy.

This therapy essentially involves application of warm medicated oil over the body according to a prescribed procedure, as a result of which the patient perspires uniformly.

Like the earlier therapy, religious rites are performed before starting this therapy. The patient is made to sit over the wooden table details of which are already described earlier. In Ayurveda, this is called *Taila-Droṇi*. Depending upon the strength of the patient and the diseases he is suffering from, the physician has to select appropriate oil for this therapy. Like the earlier therapy, a piece of clean cloth has to be tied on the head of the patient at the level of the eye-brows, to prevent flowing down of the oil (to be poured) from the head to the eyes which may cause irritation to the eyes and give rise to a feeling of discomfort to the patient. This therapy is given to both healthy persons and patients. In the case of healthy persons, it causes rejuvenation of the body and helps in the preservation and promotion of positive health. In the case of patients, it cures several diseases, details of which will be discussed later.

For a healthy person, generally, a mixture of the sesame oil and cow's ghee is used. Oils medicated by cooking with drugs for rejuvenating effects are also used in this therapy. The oil which will be most suitable for the person has, of course, to be selected by an expert physician. The duration or the course of treatment may vary depending upon the nature of the disease and the physical as well as mental conditions of the patient.

The person should be made to sit on the wooden table and four attendants should sit (or stand) – two on each side – of the table to perform massage. The medicated oil has to be made tolerably warm. With the help of pieces of cloth: 50 cm. x 50 cm. in size, the oil should be taken out of the oil pan and the cloth should be squeezed over the body of the patient by the masseurs with their hands. The pouring of the oil can also be performed with the help of specially prepared jars with a narrow mouth through which the oil comes out uniformly from the pot. The oil is to be poured over the body of the patient with uniform and medium speed. It should be neither too quickly nor too slowly poured and it should be poured from a moderate height. First of all, the medicated oil has to be applied over the head and then over the body. For application over the head, the oil should be of room temperature and for the body, it should be luke-warm. Thereafter, the pouring should be performed gently. The pouring of the warm oil over the body should be continued till the body starts perspiring on the forehead, chest and arm-pit. The attendants while applying the oil in the above manner should, at the same time, massage the body of the patient gently with their left hands. This pouring of the oil should be done only after the attendants have examined the actual heat of the oil through their own hands, in order to ensure that excessively heated oil is not poured over the body or the skin of the patient. Apart from the feeling of discomfort and excessive warmth, excessively hot oil may cause scald.

The cloth pieces are dipped into the oil pan, which is kept over the oven with very mild fire. The heat of the oil could then be tested by the hand of the masseurs and then, this should be poured (squeezed) over the body of the patient. The massage should always be from upwards to downwards. The process of massage is done in all the seven postures of the patient, as has already been described for the earlier therapy. Generally, 1½ hours to 2 hours time is required for one therapy. It takes roughly half a minute for the oil to penetrate through the skin of the patient and gradually it penetrates into all the seven groups of tissue elements of the body.

The pouring of the oil over the head should be done from a height of 8 cm. from the level of the head. Over the remaining parts of the body, pouring should be done from a height of 20 cm..

If very hot oil is applied over the body, it may give rise to burning sensation, erysipelas, fainting, fatigue, hoarseness of voice, pain in joints, vomiting, haemorrhage, fever and urticaria. The oil which is used for this therapy can be collected through the vessels, kept below the holes of the table and this oil can be repeatedly used for the same patient for 3 times more. Thereafter, fresh oil should be used for the patient. If, however, the patient can afford the expenditure, it is always better to use fresh oil every day.

The patient at times, feels completely exhausted after this therapy. In that case, he should be fanned and some cold water should be sprinkled over his body; he should be made to take rest and then he should be allowed to get up. Thereafter, the body should be massaged and excess oil from the body should be taken out with the help of a dry and clean towel. Thereafter, fresh oil is again applied to the head and the body and the flour of black gram or chick-pea is sprinkled over the body and again cleaned to take out the excess of oil. The powder of soap-nut and hot water is also used to take out the excess of oil from the body. Then, the patient should be asked to take bath. The water for bath should be boiled with the leaves of medicinal plants. The water for the head should be of the room temperature and the water for the body should be luke-warm. Bath should be taken with the help of attendants. After the bath, he is to be dressed with clean and dry cloth. Thereafter, he may be given water boiled with dried ginger and coriander to drink. If the patient feels hungry, he may be given some light and liquid food. The preparation should be boiled by adding digestive and carminative herbs. There will be some restrictions on his diet and regimen during the course of therapy and for an equal number of days thereafter. The patient should have absolute control over the body and mind and should avoid sexual intercourse altogether to get the best benefits of this therapy. He should be physically and mentally calm and quiet.

The duration of treatment will vary depending upon the strength of the patient and the disease he is suffering from. It should be done daily or at an interval of 1, 2, 3 or 4 days. Generally, one course involves administration of this therapy for 14 days. For a patient suffering from diseases caused by *vāyu* and *kapha*, the oil should be luke-warm. The oil for the head, of course, should be of room temperature. For a patient suffering from the diseases caused by *pitta*, the oil should be only slightly hot in temperature or it may be of room temperature even for the body.

In the place of medicated oil, medicated milk or sour vinegar can also be used. If milk or sour vinegar is to be used for this therapy, then, every day fresh milk and vinegar should be taken.

13

ŚIRODHĀRĀ OR POURING OIL, etc. OVER THE HEAD

It is one of the excellent therapies for the treatment of several diseases connected with head, neck, eyes, ears, nose, throat and nervous system. Its therapeutic utility for giving cure to patients suffering from long-standing insomnia and psyzophrenia is well-known. It is also used along with the other medicines for patients suffering from epileptic fits. During this therapy, medicated oil, milk or butter-milk is poured on the forehead between the eye-brows in a continuous stream. If oil is used, this therapy is called *Taila dhārā*. If milk is used for this therapy, then it is called *Dugda dhārā*. If, however, butter-milk is used for administering this therapy, then it is called *Takra dhārā*.

14

TAILA DHĀRĀ

The patient is made to lie on his back on a wooden table specially prepared for this therapy. Generally, the table used for *Navarakizhi* is used for this purpose. First of all, the head of the patient is smeared with medicated oil. Thereafter, the body of the patient is also massaged with this oil. The patient's head is made to rest over a slightly elevated position preferably over a pillow covered with rubber or plastic linen. Before beginning the therapy, some religious rites are required to be performed. The oil to be used for this therapy has to be selected by the physician depending upon the nature of the disease of the patient. Generally, two attendants are needed for this therapy. One of them should hold the vessel containing the liquid, so that the drip falls exactly on the forehead between the two eye-brows and the other collects the oil from the vessel kept below and puts it again on the oil vessel from where the oil comes in drips.

For keeping the oil, milk or butter-milk, a vessel is specially prepared. Generally, a wide mouthed earthern basin having a capacity of about 2.5 litres is used for this purpose. The basin should be shallow about 15 cm. deep, wide-mouthed, having a bottom with curvature. It should be smooth, both inside and outside and strong enough to bear the stress and strain of the oil and its handling by the attendants. It can be made of baked-mud, glass, gold, silver, wood, porcelain or stainless steel (- vide Figs. 10 to 12).

Through strings or metallic chains, it should be tied round its brim near the mouth and hanged over the head of the patient from the roof or from a specially designed stand. A small hole is made at the bottom of this basin – the size of the hole should be about one cm. in diameter or just sufficient to admit the tip of the little finger of the patient. Over the hole, a small semi-spherical hollow cup should be placed. Traditionally, a hard shell of the coconut is used for this purpose. But this cup can also be prepared of baked mud or of metal. Over the top of this cup, there should be a hole corresponding to the hole at the bottom of the basin. This cup should be placed over the basin with its mouth downwards. Through the hole of the cup, a wick with a string of thread with a free end and of about 10 cm. long should be passed. The thread of the wick should also pass through the hole at the botton of the basin. The thread of the wick should be tied firmly with a knot at the top and inserted through the hole, so that it does not slip off during the therapy and it should be loose enough to permit continuous and regular flow of the liquid that is poured into the basin for treatment. Instead of a knot, traditionally a piece of wood is inserted at the top of the cotton thread to keep it fixed and not to allow it to fall down.

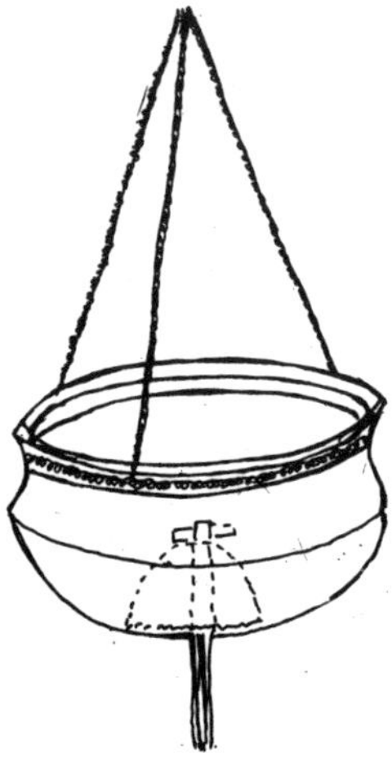

FIG. 10: Vessel for *Dhārā* Therapy (Traditional)

The basin is hanged with the help of strings from the roof of the room through a hook or from a stand specially designed for this purpose. The end of the cotton thread should be just 8 cm. above the forehead of the patient. To ensure this, the strings holding the basin should be slightly adjusted. Thereafter, the liquid is poured into the basin and is made to flow through the cotton thread continuously on the appropriate part of the forehead. The oil which comes out of the forehead of the patient is collected in a vessel kept below the table and the same is again recycled to the basin. Now a days, for convenience, a different type of vessel is used (- vide Fig. 10).

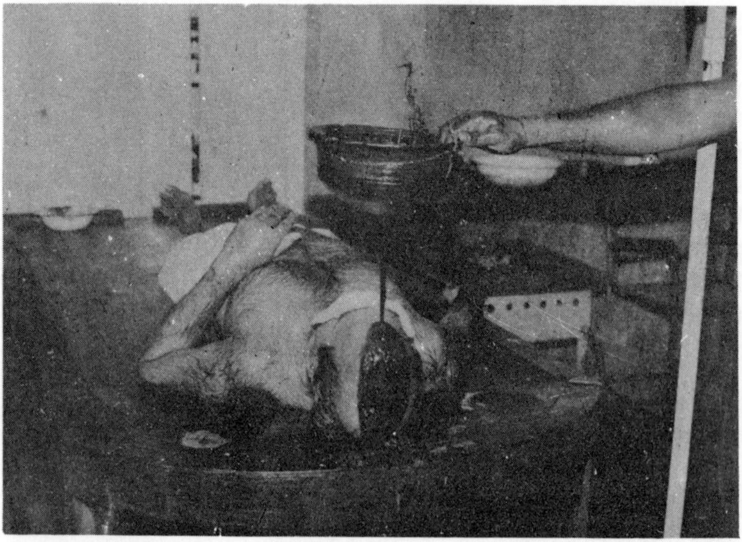

FIG 11: *Dhārā* of the head

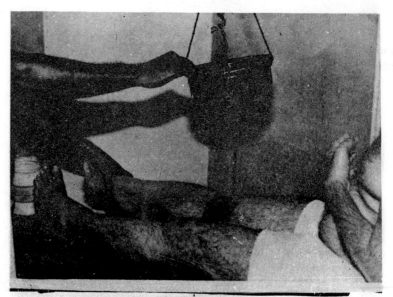

FIG 12: *Dhārā* can be given to only a part of the body

The process continues for about 1½ hrs. Throughout the therapy, the patient should lie down on his back and should not move his body. This therapy is given daily for about seven to fourteen days depending upon the nature of the disease and physical as well as mental conditions of the patient.

This therapy is better administered in the early morning and should never he given in the afternoon or at night.

Manufacture of Medicated Oil

To prepare medicated oil for *Taila dhārā* therapy, generally the following procedure is adopted. One kilogram of the root of *balā (Sida rhombifolia)* is added with 16 litres of water, boiled and reduced to 1/4th. The decoction is thren filtered out. To this decoction, one litre of sesame oil and 250 gms. of the paste of the root of *balā* is added. The oil is then cooked over mild fire. When the paste becomes sticky, one litre of cow's milk is added to it and further boiled till the paste becomes rough to touch when rolled between two fingers. If this paste is placed over the flame, then there will be no cracking noise. The cooking vessel is then removed from the oven and allowed to cool down. Thereafter, the oil is taken out by filtering and squeezing out the paste. This medicated oil is generally used for *Taila dhārā* therapy. Traditionally, some physicians use cow's ghee in the place of sesame oil in this preparation for better therapeutic results. If this medicated ghee is used in this therapy then it is called *Ghṛta dhārā*.

For different types of ailments different other types of medicated oil are used in this therapy. Their general method of preparation and recipes are given in Appendix I.

15

DUGDHA DHĀRĀ

Instead of medicated oil, milk can also be used for this therapy. For this purpose, about two litres of cow's milk should be added with eight litres of water. In it, 50 gms. of each of *balā (Sida rhombifolia)* and the thick root of *śatāvarī (Asparagus racemosus)* should be added. These roots should be cleaned properly and crushed into small pieces, kept in a thin and strong cloth and loosely tied with the help of a string in the form of bolus. In this bolus form, these roots are to be added to the milk diluted with water and placed over the oven till it is reduced to about two litres. Then, it is cooled. When it is cool enough to handle, the bundle of *balā* and *śatāarī* should be taken out and squeezed with the help of fingers and removed out of the pot. Now, the milk is ready for use for the therapy. The milk should now be cooled. If required, it should be stirred to make it cool. All the cream formed at the surface of the cooling milk should be removed. It is then added with about two litres of water from tender coconut and used for the therapy.

Before administering this therapy, the head and the body of the patient should be anointed with medicated oil and then given massage. The milk alone, without adding the coconut water can also be used for this therapy.

This is very useful for persons suffering from insanity, sleeplessness, burning sensation, giddiness and paralysis agitans.

In the place of cow's milk, milk collected from a lady (human breast-milk) can also be used in this therapy with considerable advantage. It is specially used in the cases of delirium, sleeplessness, unconsciousness and chronic fever. To one litre of human milk, one gram of camphor should be added. As in the case of *Taila dhārā*, the body of the patient should be anointed with medicated oil before administering this therapy. But if this therapy is given to a patient suffering from typhoid fever, then his head and body should bot be anointed and no massage is to be given. After pouring this milk over the forehead of the patient for one or two hours, the head of the patient should be cleaned with the help of a dry and clean cloth (towel). The patient, after this therapy, should be allowed to take rest for about one hour before resuming his work.

16

TAKRA DHĀRĀ

Two kilograms of the pulp of *āmalakī (Emblica officinalis)* should be boiled by adding eight litres of water till it is reduced to one litre. The decoction is then strained through a cloth and added with one litre of butter-milk. For preparing butter-milk, half a litre of cow's milk should be boiled, added with fermenting material and kept overnight. To this, half a litre of water is added and churned till the butter portion of it comes out. The butter is then taken out and only the liquid portion is used in this therapy added with the decoction of *āmalakī*.

Before administering this therapy, the head and the body of the patient should be anointed with medicated oil.

Traditionally, one litre of cow's milk is added with four litres of water. To this, 50 gms. of the crushed tubers of *mustā (Cyperus rotundus)* which is tied in a cloth in the form of a bolus, is added. After boiling, the milk is reduced to 1 litre, the pot is then removed from the oven. The bundle of *mustā*-powder is then squeezed to take out all the liquid from it and added to the milk. The same milk is then allowed to cool down. Into this milk, when it is slightly warm, some sour butter-milk is added and kept overnight. Next morning, the decoction of *āmalakī (Emblica officinalis)* is added to it and churned till the fat portion of it comes out. It is then strained through a cloth and used for the therapy.

This therapy is given to the patient daily for about 10 minutes.

This type of *dhārā* therapy cures the premature graying of hair, fatigue, instability in gait, headache, giddiness, aching pain and burning sensation in the palms and soles of the feet. It helps in proper functioning of the joints. It is very useful for different types of heart diseases and diseases of the eyes, ears, nose and throat. It promotes digestion and corrects anorexia, vomiting and lack of appetite. It also promotes eye-sight and cures cataract in its early stage. It is an excellent cure for chronic insomnia (sleeplessness) and often the patient who had no sleep for years together tends to get sound sleep on the table even while administering the therapy.

17

ŚIROBASTI
(Oleation of Head)

Keeping oil over the head with the help of a tubular leather cap (sac) is called *śiro-basti*.

Method of Administration

For this purpose, a tubular cap with both the ends open should be prepared of soft leather of cow or buffalo. It should be 15 cm. in length and its circumference should be according to the head of the patient. Arrangement should be made for minor adjustments of this circumference to suit the heads of different sizes. However, caps for young patients and adults should be different. One of the ends of this cap should be fitted around the head upto level of the ears. To make it tight, belt should be used.

After the patient's body is cleansed by the administration of emetic therapy etc., the patient should be given oleation and fomentation therapies. Then, he should be made to sit over a stool having the height up to his knees. Thereafter, the cap should be placed over his head. Then, with the help of the belt, it should be made tight. The flour of black gram should be made to a paste by adding warm water. This paste should be applied inside the cap over the head (the joint between the wall of the cap and the scalp) to prevent leakage of oil. Over this, the oil medicated by cooking with appropriate drugs should be poured when it is luke-warm. The level of this medicated oil should be up to 2 cm. above the hair-root. This medicated oil should be kept over the head till the patient exudes oily substance from the face, ears and nose, and till he gets relief from his painful symptoms. Approximately, the patient suffering from *vātika* diseases will need to keep this oil for 10,000 seconds; those suffering from *paittika* and *raktaja* diseases should keep it for 8,000 seconds and those suffering from *kaphaja* diseases should retain the oil for 6,000 seconds. A healthy person should retain oil for 1,000 seconds.

Thereafter, the oil should be taken out of the cap and then the belt, the paste of black gram and the cap should be removed. Thereafter, the head, shoulders, neck and back should be given gantle massage. The patient should then be given bath with luke-warm water. Wholesome diet should then be given to him. This therapy sould be repeated daily for three, five or seven days.

Therapeutic Utility

Śirobasti is useful in curing the following ailments:

(1) Facial paralysis.
(2) Sleeplessness.
(3) Dryness of mouth.
(4) Dryness of nose.
(5) Cataract.
(6) Headache and other head diseases.

18

PRECAUTIONS AND REGIMENS

Preparation of the Patient

One week before the actual treatment begins, the patient should be given a daily dose of light laxative to keep his bowels clean. This will help proper nourishment of the tissues and removal of waste products from the body. This preparatory treatment is essential, both for the healthy persons, to whom this therapy is administered for the purpose of rejuvenation and for patients to cure them of their diseases.

During the course of treatment and for an equal number of days thereafter, the patient should take proper diet, drinks and he should be free from physical as well as mental exertion.

Water for Drinking and Bath

For the purpose of drinking, water boiled with coriander, dry ginger and cumin-seeds should be used. After boiling, water should be cooled and then given to the patient to drink. For the purpose of both–cleaning the body and washing, the patient should use luke-warm water. Properties of different types of water are given in Appendix-I.

Conduct and Regimens

The patient should abstain from sexual intercourse – even the thought of sex should not come to his mind. Therefore, he should meet only the males or females of old age, who are not likely to arouse sexual passion. Suppression of natural urges should be strictly prohibited. Whenever he feels like going to toilet, he should do so without any inhibition. He should not undertake any strenuous physical exercise. His mind should be free from excitement, grief, etc.

He should avoid strong heat of the sun, strong wind, cold wind, snow and dust. Riding over the elephants, horses and fast-moving vehicles, walking over long distances, too much of speaking and talking in loud voice should be avoided. Sleeping during day time, keeping awake till late at night, sitting and standing continously for a long time should be avoided. His pillow should be neither too thick nor too thin and neither too hard nor too soft and this should be used during the sleep at night.

Diet

The patient, during the course of the therapy and for an equal number of days thereafter, should take light food at regular intervals. The ingredients, which are liquid or in semi-solid form, which are warm and which do not cause any burning sensation should be given to the patient. In addition to the quality, it is very essential to see that the patient takes his food in appropriate quantities. After the patient feels satisfied with his food, he should not continue eating. As a general rule, half the capacity of the stomach should be filled with the solid, liquid or semi-liquid food, ¼th of the capacity of stomach should be filled with water and the remaining ¼th capacity of the stomach should be kept empty. Food ingredients which are too spicy or too sour, should be avoided. He should take pulses like moong, and masoor, vegetables, milk and soups. Non-vegetarians can use meat of animals and birds living in arid zone. The meat and vegetables can be boiled or baked and they should not be fried or deep-fried. Pork and sea-fish should not be given to the patient. Care should be taken to see that the patient does not take milk or milk products along with the meat or meat preparations.

Bread and other products of wheat flour should be avoided. He should, as far as possible, use whole wheat products and good quality of rice. He should not use goat-milk, polished rice, tapioca, sweet potato, corn, chillies and tamarind. Whole corn meals, plantain, black pepper, bitter gourd, snake-gourd and *sūraṇa* are useful for him.

Cream, butter, ghee and oil should be used by him in less quantities. Ground-nut oil is strictly prohibited. He should not use other types of animal fat. Olive oil is good for the patient.

Fruits like ripe banana, pomegranate, orange, grapes and *āmalakī* are very useful for the patient.

Importance of Proper Bowel Movement

Stool is not only the refuge or the waste product of the ingredients of food, which a person takes but it also contains a considerable quantity of metabolic waste products, which come out from the tissues through the blood channels to the large intestine. The non-removal of the waste products of the ingredients of food itself gives rise to several painful and uncomfortable signs and symptoms. If, however, the waste products from the tissues are not eliminated properly, then this gives rise to auto-intoxication. The latter, apart from giving rise to several signs and symptoms, cause malnourishment of the tissues and this is an important factor which is to be looked into before the treatment of chronic diseases.

In Ayurveda, a lot of emphasis is laid upon the movement of bowels, because, endogenous diseases are broadly classified into two categories – one taking origin from the stomach and small intestine, and the other taking origin from the colon. Chronic diseases like rheumatic and rhueumatoid arthritis, gout, bronchial asthma, psoriasis, heart diseases, high bood pressure, sleeplessness, Parkinson's disease, hemiplegia and migraine are some of the commonly occurring diseases because of the impairment of the functioning of the colon. For their correction, it is necessary that the bowel movement should be regulated and if there is constipation, it should be immediately removed. If the waste products from the tissues are not properly and timely eliminated, this will enhance the ageing process and any rejuvenation therapy for the preservation and promotion of positive health, and prevention of the diseases, will not be effective in this condition.

The main signs and symptoms of chronic constipation are headache, giddiness, drowsiness, fatigue, anxiety, nervous irritability, flatulence, foul-breath, offensive perspiration, suppression of appetite, sleeplessness and coated tongue.

Depending upon the nature of the food a person takes, the bowel movement should be at least once or twice daily. Persons accustomed to vegetarian food should pass stool twice daily and those accustomed to non-vegetarian food should pass stool atleast once per day. The consistency of the stool should be semi-solid, brownish-yellow in colour and it should move out of the anus without much effort and without any pain or blood from the tract. This bowel movement is impaired if a person is mentally strained and if he has to remain awake at night for a long time. Irregular intake of food also gives rise to constipation. Intake of excess of tea, coffee, alcohol or chemical drugs often lead to the impairment of the functioning of the liver, which gives rise to constipation. Before administering Massage therapy to a patient either for curing his disease or for the purpose of rejuvenation, it is essential to see that his bowels are moving normally. If there is constipatiton, he should be given a laxative or a purgative as per the condition and strength of the patient, for proper bowel movement. Even medicated enema can be used for this purpose. Traditionally, a decoction called *Gandharvahastādi kaṣāya* is given to the patient for 2-3 days before the administration of Massage therapy for evacuation of the accumulated bowels from the colon and accumulated waste products from the tissues. He should be given water to drink in liberal quantity. Ingredients which cause dryness in the body should be avoided. Regular intake of milk helps in the removal of the constipation. Ghee and milk helps in removal of the constipation. Ghee, butter and almond oil are very useful for such patients. Along with food, ghee, etc. should be given to the patient to take.

Generally, a thin gruel of rice and moong dal (popularly known as *khichri*) added with liberal quantity of cow's ghee is to be given to the patient prior to the administration of Massage therapy as a preparatory measure.

Even during the course of therapy and thereafter, the physician should take care that the patient's bowels are moving freely. Otherwise, the therapy is not likely to produce the desired result or effect.

Drinks

The patient should take water and milk, fruit juice and soups in adequate quantities during the course of the therapy. Whenever he feels thirsty, he should be given suitable drinks. Water boiled by adding coriander, dry ginger and cumin seeds should be cooled and kept ready in earthern pots for the convenience of the patient. He should take about 3-5 litres of water per day during and after the meals.

Drinking excess of water in the evening or at night may stimulate the kidney and may cause frequent urination of the patient at night, which may disturb his sleep. Therefore, excess water should, as far as possible, be avoided at night and even in the evenings. The kidneys should, as far as possible, be given rest at night and that will not affect the sleep of the patient. During the Massage therapy, good sleep is very very essential.

It should be kept in mind that the patient should not be given tea and coffee during this therapy. Alcoholic preparations, tobacco and intoxicating drugs are strictly prohibited.

Sleep

Proper sleep is very essential for the patient to make the Massage therapy produce the desired results or effects. He should go to bed earlier at night and get up from the bed earlier in the morning. The Massage therapy itself will promote sound sleep. Because of fatigue, the patient may like to sleep during the day time. It should be strictly avoided. Sleep, during day time, will produce many adverse effects on the patient's body and mind. If he wants, he can take rest for about an hour during day time, but he should never sleep at that time.

Clothing

Depending upon the geographical and climatic conditions, the patient should use appropriate warm or ordinary clothing. But it should be kept in view that the clothing should be light and the patient should avoid clothings prepared of synthetic fibres which prevent proper perspiration from the body and liberation of obnoxious material through the sweat. The patient should never sleep bare-bodied. He should wear cotton or silken apparel. The under-garments should be light and loose preferably made from cotton. There should not be any obstruction to the process of circulation in the body during the course of the therapy for which tight shirt or tight belt should be avoided.

Exercise

During the course of the therapy, the patient should take light exercise which will improve the circulation of blood among the tissues of his body. This will help in the removal of waste products from the tissues and provide proper nourishment to them.

During the Massage therapy, tissucs of the body undergo

tremendous change. These are revitalised. The patient may feel a little fatigued. The weight of the patient may come down a little. Therefore, during this transitional period and during the stage of the reconditioning of the tissues, one should strictly avoid violent exercises. If he exposes himself to hard work, then, this may give rise to neurasthenia and neuralgia. Violent exercise may also give rise to heart diseases, high blood pressure, fever and tuberculosis. Thus, the very purpose of Massage therapy will be defeated. The practice of *āsanas* (physical postures) and *prāṇāyāma* (breathing exercises) prescribed in Yogic texts, are very useful for the patient during the course of this therapy.

Study

Excessive reading may give rise to strain in the eyes and the mind. It should be remembered that eyes along with the other parts of the body are already weak during this course of this therapy. Therefore, excessive reading should be avoided. Reading of light material, particularly religious scriptures and books is very useful. But even this religious and light study should be for a limited period. The patient should not read exciting novels or erotic literature, because, it will produce several adverse effects on his body and mind. The reading should be performed in appropriate light keeping the book or scripture at an appropriate distance from the eyes. Reading newspapers and/or journals should be encouraged.

Fresh Air

During the course of this therapy, the body tissues undergo the process of reconstruction, nourishment and rejuvenation. For this aim to be achieved, it is necessary that the room of the patient where he sleeps, sits or rests, should have adequate quantities of fresh air. Even in winter, the room should not be made air-tight. Air-conditioning of the room of the patient should, as far as possible, be avoided. If because of climatic conditions, air-conditioning is necessary, it should be ensured that the room gets adequate fresh air and it is neither too hot nor too cold. As far as possible, the patient should be close to the nature and should avoid artificial way of living. It is necessary, however, that the room should be free from smoke, dust, strong wind and excess of moisture. Making the room excessively cold during the summer will give rise to several painful signs and symptoms. On the other hand, making the room very hot during winter, will prevent the rejuvenation of the tissues.

Friends and Attendants

As has been mentioned before, during the course of the treatment and for an equal number of days thereafter, the patient should avoid sexual intercourse. Even the thought of sex might give rise to several diseases, during this period. Therefore, the friends and attendants of the patient should be generally of the same sex as that of the patient and only the senior relatives of the patient even of opposite sex can meet him and discuss with him. Cheerfulness has some invigorating effect on his body and the mind. Friends and associates whom the patient normally desires to attend on him, should keep him happy and cheerful. The patient should not be given any exciting or sorrowful news during the course of the therapy.

Environment of the patient's place of residence should be, as far as possible, pleasant to the eyes and the mind. Hospitals for this type of therapy should, therefore, be constructed in a garden or on a hill-top or on sea-shore, in an isolated place. The noise of vehicles or people around the hospital should be limited to the barest minimum.

Bath

During the course of the therapy and for an equal number of days thereafter, the patient should take bath in slightly warm water. The temperature of the water should be slightly above that of the body of the patient. He should not avoid bath. Taking bath in cold water should be strictly avoided. This may give rise to pain in joints. Bath in excessively warm water will make the patient very weak. During the bath, the body of the patient should be massaged with a towel and after the bath, it should be properly cleaned with the help of a dry towel. This will promote proper blood circulation and elimination of waste products from the tissues.

Water for bath should better be boiled by adding the barks and leaves of the following trees:

i. *Śigru (Moringa pterigosperma)*
ii. *Eraṇḍa (Ricinus communis)*

iii. *Karañja (Pongamia pinnata)*
iv. *Surasā (Ocimum sanctum)*
v. *Śirīṣa (Albizzia lebbeck)*
vi. *Arka (Calotropis procera)*
vii. *Mālatī (Aganosma dichotoma)*
viii. *Dhaturā (Datura metel)*
ix. *Panasa (Artocarpus heterophyllus)*

The leaves or barks of these plants are to be collected fresh, cut into small pieces and boiled by adding 30 times by weight of water. It should be boiled till it is reduced to half of the original quantity (15 litres). Then, the leaves should be removed. One third of this water is to be taken in another pot and made to cool. Cooled water should be used for giving bath to the head of the patient. The body of the patient should, however, be bathed with luke-warm water. Warm water should not be used for head. This will cause impairment of the eye-sight.

For giving proper bath, the patient should be assisted by some assistants/attendants for removing excess of oil from the head and the body. Flour of black gram, green gram or chick-pea or soap-nut should be used for this purpose.

Bath should be given to the head first and then the body should be washed. The head should then be cleaned and dried with the help of a dry towel. Thereafter, the body should be wiped out by the dry towel. The water to be used for the head should not be escessively cold. If that happens, then the patient will suffer from cold, cough, pneumonia and possibly fever. If the patient is already suffering from cold, cough etc., then slightly luke-warm water can be used for head-bath also.

Other Regimens

The patient should avoid watching the television. Light music is very useful for the patient, during the course of the treatment. Reciting the *Mantra 'Oṃ'* mentally during the period of rest is very useful. Other religious *mantras* and incantations can also be recited mentally during this period.

Suitable Time

The best season (time) for this therapy is when the climate is neither too hot nor too cold and there is not much of humidity in the atmosphere. Autumn and spring seasons are very suitable for this therapy. But in countries where the temperature is very low or very high, this therapy can be administered to a patient with appropriate air-conditioning arrangements. However, if a patient suffers from a serious disease, which justifies immediate administration of Massage therapy, then one need not bother about the weather, and while taking proper care to maintain the temperature of the therapy-room and in his bed-room, the therapy can be administered during any part of the year.

Course of Treatment

Massage, as been mentioned before, should be performed daily before taking bath for preservation and promotion of positive health. Massage as a special therapy, has to be administered for a limited period depending upon the nature of the disease and the condition of the patient. Each course can vary from 7-14 days. The therapy can be administered every day or on alternate days or after a gap of two days depending upon the nature of the disease and the strength of the patient.

Suppression of Natural Urges *(Vega-rodha)*

During the process of digestion and metabolism, several types of waste products are produced. Some of these are utilised in the body and some others are required to be eliminated through different channels. Appropriate and timely elimination of these *malas* or waste products help a person to have positive health and prevent occurence of diseases. Because of affliction by diseases, these waste products, at times, are produced in large quantities. While treating the ailments of such patients, it is essential to eliminate these morbid factors. During the normal course of living, these waste products get eliminated through different channels. But because of social and cultural inhibitions and ignorance, at times, a person is forced to suppress these natural urges as a result of which the waste products remain adhered to tissues and cause several diseases. This comes in the way of rejuvenation of tissues. Therefore, during Massage therapy and even for some more days after the therapy, the patient should be careful to avoid the suppression of these natural urges.

These natural urges are of thirteen types. Signs and symptoms produced by their suppression and the outline of the management of such ailments are described below:

(1) Urge for Micturition

Suppression of the urge for micturition causes pain in the bladder and phallus, dysuria, headache, bending of the body and distension of the lower abdomen.

If during the Massage therapy, these signs and symptoms appear as a result of suppression of the urge for urination, then the patient should be given tub-bath, massage, inhalation therapy with the help of nasal drops and medicated enema.

(2) Urge for Defecation

If a person suppresses the urge for defecation, then this causes colic pain, headache, retention of faeces and flatus, cramps in the calf-muscles and abdominal distension.

If during the course of Massage therapy, such signs and symptoms appear as a result of the suppression of the urge for defecation, then the patient should be given fomentation therapy, massage, tub-bath, suppositories, medicated enema and such food and drinks as would be having laxative effects.

(3) Urge for Seminal Discharge

During the course of Massage therapy any form of sexual intercourse is strictly prohibited. If, however, by mistake or out of ignorance, the patient gets such an urge and he suppresses the urge, then he will suffer from pain in the testicles and phallus, malaise, cardiac pain, and retention of urine.

If such signs and symptoms are manifested during the course of the Massage therapy because of seminal retention, then the patient should have massage, tub-bath and he should take *madiarā* type of wine, chicken, *śāli* type of rice, milk and medicated enema.

To avoid all these complications, the physian should ensure that the patient does not get any erotic stimulation through his friends, family members and attendants.

(4) Urge for Passing Flatus

If one suppresses the urge for passing flatus during the course of the Massage therapy, then he suffers from retention of faeces, urine and flatus, abdominal distension, pain in abdomen, fatigue and such other abdominal disorders.

If such signs and symptoms are manifested during the course of massage, then the patient should be given oleation and fomentation therapies and suppositories, and he should take food and drinks having carminative effects. Such a patient should be given medicated enema.

(5) Urge for Emesis

If a person suppresses the urge for vomiting, then he suffers from pruritus, urticaria, anorexia, black pigmentation of the face, oedema, anemia, fever, skin diseases, nausea and erysipelas.

If such signs and symptoms appear in a patient during the course of Massage therapy, then he should be given emetic therapy, smoking, fasting and blood-letting therapies, and he should take ununctuous food and drinks, physical exercise and purgation therapy.

(6) Urge for Sneezing

During the course of Massage therapy, if a person suppresses the urge for sneezing, then he suffers from torticolis, headache, facial paralysis, hemicrania and weakness of the sense organs.

If such signs and symptoms appear during the course of Massage therapy, the patient should be given fomentation therapy in the head and neck region. He should be administered Smoking therapy and nasal drops. He should be given such food and drinks which will alleviate *vāyu* in his body.

(7) Urge for Eructation

If the patient, during the course of Massage therapy, suppresses the urge for eructation, then he suffers from hiccup, dyspnoea, anorexia, tremor, obstacles in the functioning of the heart and lungs.

If such signs and symptoms appear in the patient, then he should be given therapies prescribed for the treatment of hiccup.

(8) Urge for Yawning

If the patient, during the course of Massage therapy, suppresses the urge for yawning, then he suffers from convulsions, contractions in the musculature, numbness, tremor and trembling in the body.

If such signs and symptoms appear in the patient, then he should be given such therapies including drugs, diet and drinks as would alleviate *vāyu*.

(9) Urge for Hunger

If a patient, during the course of Massage therapy, suppresses the urge of hunger, then he suffers from emaciation, weakness, change in the bodily complexion, malaise, anorexia and giddiness.

Such a patient should be given unctuous, hot and light food.

(10) Urge for Drinking Liquids (Thirst)

If the patient, during the course of Massage therapy, suppresses the urge of thirst, then he suffers from dryness of the mouth and throat, deafness, exhaustion, weakness and cardiac pain.

Such a patient should be given cooling and nourishing (refreshing) drinks.

(11) Urge for Weeping (Tears)

If a person during the course for Massage therapy, suppresses the urge for crying (tears), then he suffers from rhinitis, eye-diseases, heart diseases, anorexia and giddiness.

In that event, the patient should be made to take sound sleep. He might be given alcoholic drink to overcome the grief and he should be consoled.

During the course of Massage therapy, all precautions should be taken not to communicate any sorrowful news to the patient. His friends, relatives and attendants should be cautioned about it in advance.

(12) Urge for Sleep

If the patient, during the course of Massage therapy, suppresses the urge for going to sleep, then he suffers from yawning, malaise, drowsiness, headache and heaviness of the eyes.

If the patient suffers from such signs and symptoms, then he should be administered such therapies as would produce sound sleep.

(13) Urge for Breathing

If during the course of Massage therapy, the patient suppresses the urge for breathing specially for deep-breathing, after exhaustion or exercise, then he suffers from phantom tumour, heart diseases and fainting.

In such an event, the patient should be given sufficient rest and he should be given such therapies including drugs, food and drinks as would alleviate *vāyu*.

These precautions including diet, drinks and regimens should always be kept in view while administering different types of special Massage therapies for the purpose of rejuvenation of the body and prevention as well as cure of obstinate and otherwise incurable diseases.

APPENDIX-I

PROPERTIES OF IMPORTANT INGREDIENTS USED IN MASSAGE THERAPY[1]

TAILA (OIL IN GENERAL)

Taste: Sweet.
Attributes: Heavy, *sara* (fluid) and non-slimy.
Potency: Hot.
Vipāka: Sweet.
(Taste which emerges after digestion)

Specific action: Laxative, aphrodisiac and promoter of *sthairya* (steadiness), *bala* (strength) and *varṇa* (complexion).

Uṣṇa Taila (Hot Oil)

Taste: Bitter.
Subsidiary Taste: Astringent.
Attribute: Sharp.
Vipāka: Sweet.
Specific action: Nourishing and alleviator of *kapha* and *vāyu*.
Therapeutic usage: Cures *rakta pitta* (a condition characterised by bleeding from different parts of the body).

Lepana (External Application of Sesame Oil)

Action: Digestive stimulant.
Specific action: Promotes intellect and hair, and cleanses the skin and uterus.
Therapeutic usage: Cures exhausion, *meha* (obstinate urinary diseases including diabetes), diseases of ears, *yoni* (female genital tract) and eyes and headache. It is useful in laceration, dislocation,

---

1. Prepared on the basis of Materia Medica of Ayurveda based on *Madanapāla Nighaṇṭu* Pub: B. Jain Publishers, New Delhi, 1991.

excision and fracture of bones and biting by wild animals, *viṣa* (poisoning), injury and burn by fire.

Note: Sesame oil is always wholesome in above diseases if taken internally. It is also used externally for massage.

Ghee and Til Oil

Boiled ghee loses its potency after one year. But oil whether boiled or not, maintains its potency for a long period. Therefore, it is better than ghee.

Eraṇḍa Taila (Castor Oil)

Taste: Sweet.
Subsidiary taste: Astringent.
Attributes: *Sūkṣma* (subtle).
Potency: Hot.
Action: *Dīpana* (digestive stimulant).
Specific action: Purgative, aphrodisiac, useful for skin, promoter of longevity, intellect, complexion and strength, and alleviator of *vāyu*.
Therapeutic usage: Cures *udara* (obstinate abdominal diseases including ascites), *ānāha* (flatulence), *gulma* (phantom tumour), *aṣṭhīlā* (hard tumour in the abdomen), *kaṭi graha* (stiffness of lumber region), *vāta śoṇita* (gout), *śūla* (colic pain), *vraṇa* (ulcer), *śotha* (oedema), *āma* (a product of improper digestion and metabolism) and *vidradhi* (abscess).

It cleanses the *yoni* (vagina) and *śukra* (semen).

Kaṭu Taila (Oils having Pungent Taste)

The oil extracted from *pṛthvīkā, mūla, jīmūtā, dantī, kavaca, śigru, nimba, atasī, karañja, arka, hastikarṇa, iṅgudī, śaṅkhinī, nīpa, kampilla, bilva, jyotiṣmatī, kusumbha, sarṣapa* and *suvarcalā*:

Taste: Bitter.
Attributes: Light and sharp.
Potency: Hot.
Vipāka: Pungent.

Specific action: Laxative and alleviators of *kapha*.
Therapeutic usage: Cure *kuṣṭha* (obstinate skin diseases including leprosy), *meha* (obstinate urinary diseases including diabetes), *mūrcchā* (fainting), *mada* (intoxication) and *krimi* (parasitic infestation).

Nimba Taila (Neem Oil)

Specific action: Alleviates *kapha*.
Therapeutic usage: Cures *kuṣṭha* (obstinate skin diseases including leprosy), *vraṇa* (ulcer), *jvara* (fever) and *krimi* (parasitic infestation).

Atasī Taila (Oil from *Linum Usitatissimum*)

Attributes: Heavy and unctuous.
Potency: Hot.
Vipāka: Pungent.
Specific action: Promotes strength and power of digestion and alleviates *kapha, pitta* and *vāyu*.

Note: It is not useful for eyes.

Sārṣapa Taila (Mustard Oil)

Attribute: Light.
Therapeutic usage: Cures *kṛmi* (parasitic infestation), *kuṣṭha* (obstinate skin diseases including leprosy), *kaṇḍū* (itches), *meha* (obstinate urinary diseases including diabetes) and diseases of ear and head.

Note: It vitiates the *pitta* and blood.

Kusumbha Taila (Oil from *Carthamus Tinctorius*)

Taste: Pungent.
Attribute: Sharp.
Potency: Hot
Specific action: Promotes strength and alleviates *vāyu*.

Notes:(i) It is harmful for eyes.
(ii) It is *vidāhi* (which causes burning sensation).
(iii) It vitiates *kapha* and *pitta*.

Jyotiṣmatī Taila (Oil from *Celastrus paniculatus*)

Specific action: Promotes memory and intellect.

Note: It vitiates *pitta*.

Nārikelādi Taila (Oils of Coconut, etc.)

Oils of *akṣoṭikā, ahimuktā, akṣa (bibhītakī)* and *nārikela*:

Attribute: Heavy
Potency: Cold
Specific action: Promote hair and alleviate *pitta* and *vāyu*.

Note: They aggravate *kapha*.

Śiṃśapādi Taila (Oils of Śiṃśapā, etc.)

Oils of *śiṃśapā, aguru, gaṇḍīra, rasālā* and *aindradāru (deva dāru):*

Taste: Astringent, pungent and bitter.
Specific action: Alleviates *kapha* and *vāyu*.
Therapeutic usage: Cure *duṣṭa vraṇa* (putrid ulcer), *vāta rakta* (gout), *viṣa* (poisoning), *kaṇḍū* (itching) and *kuṣṭha* (obstinate skin diseases including leprosy).

Bhallātaka Taila *(Semecarpus anacardium)* **and Tuvaraka** *(Hydnocarpus laurifolia)* **Taila**

Taste: Sweet and bitter.
Potency: Hot.
Specific action: Alleviate all the three *doṣas*.
Therapeutic usage: Cure *kuṣṭha* (obstinate skin diseases including leprosy) located in the upper and lower parts of the body, vitiation of blood, *medas* (adiposity), *meha* (obstinate urinary diseases including diabetes) and *kṛmi* (parasitic infestation).

Pālāśa, Mādhūka and Pāṭala Taila (Oil Extracted from the fruits of *Butea monosperma, Madhuca indica* and *Stereospermum suaveolens*)

Taste: Astringent and sweet.
Specific action: Alleviate *pitta*.
Therapeutic usage: cure *dāha* (burning syndrome) and diseases caused by the aggravation of *kapha*.

Trapuṣādi Taila (Oil Extracted from Trapuṣa, etc.)

Oils of *kūṣmāṇḍa, trapuṣa, ervāru, tumbī, kāliṅga, tiktaka, priyāla, jīvantī* and *śleṣmāntaka:*

Attribute: Heavy.
Potency: Cold.
Vipāka: Sweet.
Specific action: Diuretics and alleviators of *vāyu* and *pitta*.

Notes: (i) They do not stimulate digestion.
(ii) They are *abhiṣyandi* (which obstruct the channels of circulation).
(iii) They vitiate *kapha*.

Ekaiṣija Taila

Potency: Cold.
Specific action: Alleviates *pitta*.

Note: It aggravates *kapha* and *vāyu*.

Yavatiktā Taila (Oil Extracted from *Andrographis paniculata*)

Taste: Slightly bitter.
Action: Digestive stimulant.
Specific action: Rejuvenating, promoter of intellect, *lekhana* (depleting) and alleviator of all the three *doṣas*.

Note: It is wholesome.

Āmra Taila (Oil from Mango-Seed)

Taste: Slightly bitter and sweet.
Attributes: Ununctuous and *viśada* (non-slimy).
Specific action: Alleviates *kapha* and *vāyu*.

Notes:(i) It contains good smell.
(ii) It does not vitiate *pitta* in excess.

SNEHA VARGA (FATS IN GENERAL)

All types of *sneha* (fat like butter, ghee, oil, etc.) obtained from the plants share the properties of oil. They alleviate *vāyu*.

Among them, oily substance is secondary. They promote strength and complexion.

Medas etc. (Muscle Fat and Bone-marrow)

Fat, Muscle fat and Bone-marrow of Animals Inhabiting Marshy and Arid land and of Domesticated Animals:

Taste: Sweet.
Attribute: Heavy.
Potency: Hot.
Specific action. Alleviate *vāyu*.

Fat, etc. of Mares, Carnivorous animals and Animals dwelling in Arid Land:

Taste: Astringent.
Attribute: Light.
Potency: Cold.
Therapeutic usage: Cure *rakta pitta* (a condition characterised by bleeding from different parts of the body).
Fat, etc. of Pratuda (Packer Birds) and Viṣkira (Gallinacious Birds)

Alleviate kapha.

NAVANĪTA(BUTTER)

Attribute: Light.
Specific action: Constipative.

Freshly Collected Butter

Taste: Sweet.
Attribute: Light.
Potency: Cold.
Specific action: Constipative.

Butter Preserved for some Days

Taste: Slightly astringent and sour.
Action: Stimulates digestive power.
Specific action: Aphrodisiac, promoter of eye-sight and alleviator of *pitta* and *vāyu*.
Therapeutic usage: Cures *kṣaya* (consumption), *arśas* (piles), *vraṇa* (ulcer) and *kāsa* (bronchitis).

Note: It is *avidāhi* (which does not cause burning sensation).

Butter Preserved for a Long Time

Attribute: Heavy.
Specific action: Aphrodisiac and strength promoting.
Therapeutic usage: Cures *śotha* (oedema).

Notes: (i) It is like an ambrosia for infants.
(ii) It produces *medas* (fat).
(iii) It aggravates *kapha*.

Milk-Butter or Butter Collected from Milk

Taste: Sweet.
Attributed: Extremely unctuous.
Potency: Excessively cold.
Specific action: Constipative, aphrodisiac, promoter of eye-sight and strength.
Therapeutic usage: Cures *rakta pitta* (a disease characterised by bleeding from different parts of the body).

GHṚTA (GHEE OR CLARIFIED BUTTER)

Taste: Sweet.
Attributes: Heavy and unctuous.
Potency: Cold.
Action: *Dīpana* (digestive stimulant).
Specific action: Rejuvenating, promoter of eye-sight, *kānti* (complexion), *ojas* (vital fluid), *tejas* (semen), beauty, intellect, and voice, and alleviator of *vāyu* as well as *pitta*.
Therapeutic usage: Cures *viṣa* (poisoning), *alakṣmī* (inauspiciousness), *udāvartta* (upward movement of wind in the stomach), *jvara* (fever), *unmāda* (insanity), *śūla* (colic pain), *ānāha* (constipation), *vraṇa* (ulcer), *kṣaya* (consumption), *vīsarpa* (erysipelas) and *kṣata* (injury or phthisis).

Notes: (i) It is generally useful for children and old persons.
(ii) It is very *abhiṣyandi* (which obstructs the channels of circulation).

Ghee Prepared from Milk Directly

Potency: Cold.
Specific action: Constipative and alleviator of *pitta* and *vāyu*.
Therapeutic usage: Cures eye-diseases, *dāha* (burning syndrome), vitiation of blood, *mada* (intoxication), *mūrcchā* (fainting) and *bhrama* (giddiness).

Old Ghee

Vīpāka: Pungent.
Action: *Dīpana* (digestive stimulant).
Specific action: Alleviates all the three *doṣas*.
Therapeutic usage: Cures diseases of ears and eyes, *śiraḥśūla* (headache), *kuṣṭha* (obstinate skin diseases including leprosy), *apasmāra* (epilepsy), *śotha* (oedema), *yoniroga* (ailments of female genital organ), *jvara* (fever), *śvāsa* (dyspnoea), *arśas* (piles), *gulma* (phantom tumour) and *pīnasa* (rhinitis).

Note: It is useful for *basti* (enema) and *nasya* (inhalation therapy).

Ghṛta Maṇḍa (Upper portion of the Ghee)

Attributes: Light and sharp.
Specific action: Laxative.

Note: It shares the properties of ghee.

Kaumbha Sarpi

The ghee which is preserved for more than ten years is called *kaumbha sarpi*.

Attribute: Light.
Therapeutic usage: Cures the afflictions by *rākṣas* (evil spirits).

Mahāghṛta (ghee which is preserved for more than hundred years) is the best among all the ghees, in its properties.

The qualities of ghee are similar to those of the milk of respective animals. Ghee prepared from cow's milk is the best among all the ghees and ghee prepared from sheep's milk is the most inferior among them.

DUGDHA (MILK)

Taste: Sweet.
Attributes: Heavy and unctuous.
Potency: Cold.
Specific action: Rejuvenating, life-giver, promoter of strength, intellect and tissue elements as well as alleviator of *vāyu* and *pitta*.
Therapeutic usage: Cures diseases of semen and *rakta* (blood), *śvāsa* (dyspnoea), *kṣaya* (consumption), *arśas* (piles) and *bhrama* (giddiness).

Notes: (i) Milk is useful for children, old persons and emaciated persons.
(ii) It is useful for persons who excessively indulge in sex.
(iii) It is generally wholesome for living beings.
(iv) It is specially useful for *ojas* (vital fluid).

Go-dugdha (Cow's Milk).

Teste: Sweet.
Attributes: Heavy and unctuous.
Potency: Cold.
Specific action: Rejuvenating, nourishing, life-giver, promoter of breast. Milk and complexion and alleviator of *vāyu* and *pitta*.

Notes:(i) The milk of a black cow is the best.
(ii) The milk of a white cow aggravates *kapha*, and is heavy.
(iii) The milk of the cow having a very young calf or without a calf aggravates all the three *doṣas*, namely, *vāyu, pitta* and *kapha*.

The milk of the cow which takes *piṇyāka* (cake of oil-seeds) etc. is heavy and alleviator of *kapha*.

Ajādugdha (Goat's Milk)

Goat's milk shares the properties of cow's milk. In addition, it has the following properties:

Attribute: Light.
Action: *Dīpana* (digestive stimulant).
Specific action: Constipative.
Therapeutic usage: Cures *kṣaya* (consumption), *arśas* (piles), *atīsāra* (diarrhoea), *pradara* (menorrhagia), *asra* (vitiation of blood), *bhrama* (giddiness) and *jvara* (fever).

Note:Since goats are of a small physique, they eat mostly pungent and bitter ingredients as food, they drinks very little water and they perform a lot of physical exercise, their milk cures all diseases.

Avi-Dugdha (Sheep's Milk)

Taste: Sweet.
Attributes: Heavy and unctuous.
Specific action: Promote of hair and alleviator of *vāyu* and *kapha*.
Therapeutic usage: Cures *kāsa* (bronchitis) caused by *vāyu*.

Note: It is useful in for a patient having aggravation of *vāyu*.

Mahiṣī Dugdha (Buffalo's Milk)

Taste: Sweet.
Attributes: Heavy and unctuous (it is more unctuous than cow's milk).
Specific action: Promotes strength and *śukra* (semen) and induces sleep.

Notes:(i) It is *malābhiṣyandi* (which obstructs the elimination of stool).
(ii) It suppresses the power of digestion.

Nārī Dugdha (Woman's Milk)

Attribute: Light.
Potency: Cold.
Action: Digestive stimulant.
Specific action: Alleviates *vāyu* and *pitta*
Therapeutic usage: Cures pain in the eyes and injury to the eyes.

Note: It is excellent for *nasya* (inhalation therapy) and *āścyotana* (pouring into the eyes).

Hastinī Dugdha (Elephant's Milk)

Taste: Sweet.
Attribute: Heavy.
Potency: Cold.
Specific action: Promotes eye-sight and strength.

Auṣṭra Dugdha (Camel Milk)

Taste: Sweet and saline.
Attributes: Light and ununctuous.
Action: Digestive stimulant.
Specific action: Laxative and alleviator of *kapha*.

Therapeutic usage: Cures *kṛmi* (parasitic infestation), *kuṣṭha* (obstinate skin diseases including leprosy), *ānāha* (flatulence), *śotha* (oedema) and *udara* (obstinate abdominal diseases including ascites).

Āśva Dugdha (Mare-Milk)

Taste: Sweet, saline and sour.
Attributes: Ununctuous and light.
Specific action: Promotes strength and alleviates *vāyu*.
Therapeutic usage: Cures *śoṣa* (consumption).

Note: Milk of all animals having one hoof shares the properties of mare's milk.

Properties of Dhāroṣṇa Dugdha (Milk which is warm Immediately after Milking), etc.

Attribute: Light.
Potency: Cold.
Action: Digestive stimulant.
Specific action: It promotes strength and alleviates all the three *doṣas*.

Note: This *dhāroṣṇa* milk becomes stale after three *muhūrttas* (one *muhūrta* = 48 minutes), and it kills a person like poison if taken after six *muhūrttas* (one *muhūrta* = 48 minutes). Therefore, this *dhāroṣṇa* (when it is warm immediately after milking) milk having cooling attribute should be taken immediately. It is like ambrosia. When it becomes cold after milking (*dhārāśīta*) it aggravates all the three *doṣas*, viz, *vāyu, pitta* and *kapha*.

Cow's milk is useful when it is *dhāroṣṇa* (when it is warm after milking), buffalo's milk is useful when it becomes *dhārā śīta* (cold after milking), sheep's milk is useful when it is warm after boiling and goat's milk is wholesome when it becomes cold after boiling.

Milk which is cooled after boiling alleviates *pitta* and milk which is warm after boiling alleviates *kapha* and *vāyu*.

The milk which is excessively boiled is heavy, ununctuous, *vṛṣya* (aphrodisiac) and strength promoting.

Unboiled Milk

The milk which is not boiled is heavy. It produces *āma* (a product of improper digestion and metabolism) and is *abhiṣyandi* (which obstructs the channels of circulation).

Only woman's milk is wholesome if it is not boiled. After boiling, it aggravates all the *doṣas*.

During night, the attributes of moon are predominant and there is no exercise. Therefore, milk obtained early in the morning is generally *viṣṭambhi* (wind forming), heavy and nourishing.

During day time, there is exposure to sun rays, exercise and wind. Therefore, evening milk alleviates *śrama* (fatigue), *vāyu* and *pitta*. It promotes strength and eye-sight.

Prohibited Milk

Milk whose colour is spoiled, which has become sour, which produces foul smell and which is of knotted appearance should not be used.

It should not be taken when mixed with sour things and salt, because this type of milk produces ailments like *kuṣṭha* (obstinate skin diseases including leprosy).

Santānikā

The layer of cream which is formed on the surface of milk after boiling is known as *santānikā*.

Attributes: Heavy and ununctuous.
Potency: Cold.
Specific action: Aphrodisiac and alleviator of *pitta, vāyu* and vitiated blood.

Moraṭī, Pīyūṣa, etc.

Moraṭa

After seven days of delivery, the *aprasanna* milk (which lacks in appropriate qualities) is called *maraṭa*. According to Jaiyyaṭa, the *naṣṭa* (curdled) milk which becomes like water is called *moraṭa*.

Pīyūṣaghana

The milk of the cow immediately after delivery is called *pīyūṣa ghana* (lit. thick ambrosia).

Dadhi-Kūrcikā

The preparation made out by boiling equal quantities of curd and milk is called *dadhi kūrcikā*.

Takra Kūrcitā, Kilāṭa, etc.

The preparation made out by boiling equal quantities of butter-milk and milk is called *takra kūrcikā*.

When this preparation is made out in a solid form (*piṇḍa*), it is called *kilāṭaka*.

If the above preparation is made out without boiling but by adding sugar then it is called *kṣīraśāka*.

Properties of Moraṭa, etc.

Attributes: Heavy.

Specific action: Aphrodisiac, cardiac tonic, nourishing, inducer of sleep and alleviator of *vāta* etc.

Notes:(i) They produce *āma* (a product of improper digestion and metabolism).

(ii) They aggravate *kapha*.

Takra Kūrcikā

Attribute: Ununctuous.

Specific action: Constipative.

Notes:(i) It is difficult for digestion.

(ii) It aggravates *vāyu*.

DADHI (CURD OR YOGHURT)

Dadhi and *styāna payas* – these are the synonyms of well fermented curd. If slightly fermented it is called *mandaka*.

Varieties: Curd is of four varieties: *miṣṭa* (sweet), *amla* (sour), *atyamla* (excessively sour) and *madhurāmla* (both sweet and sour in taste):

Taste: Astringent (subsidiary taste).
Attributes: Heavy and ununctuous.
Potency: Hot.
Vipāka: Sour
Action: Digestive stimulant.
Specific action: Constipative and strength promoting.
Therapeutic usage: Cures *mūtra kṛcchra* (dysuria), *pratiśyāya* (coryza), *śītāṅga* (coldness in the body), *viṣama jvara* (irregular fever), *atisāra* (diarrhoea), *aruci* (anorexia) and *kārśya* (emaciation).

Notes: (i) It vitiates *pitta, kapha* and blood.
(ii) It aggravates *śotha* (oedema) and *medas* (adiposity).
(iii) This fermented product of milk promotes strength, prosperity and auspiciousness. It it praise-worthy and an excellent food. Its sight during journey is a good omen.

Manda (Immature Curd)

It aggravates all the three *doṣas*.

Sweet Variety of Curd

It alleviates *vāyu* and *pitta*.

Sour Variety of Curd

It aggravates *kapha, pitta* and blood.

Excessively Sour Curd

It produces *rakta pitta* (a disease characterised by bleeding from different parts of the body).

Sweet and Sour Curd

It has the miscellaneous properties of different types of curd.

Properties of the Curd of Cow's Milk, etc.

Curd of Cow's Milk

Attribute: Unctuous.
Vipāka: Sweet.
Action: Digestive stimulant.
Specific action: An excellent promoter of strength, appetite and nourishment and alleviator of *vāyu*.

It is sacred.

Curd of Goat's Milk

Attribute: Light.
Action: Digestive stimulant.
Specific action: Constipative and alleviator of all the three *doṣas*.
Therapeutic usage: Cures *śvāsa* (dyspnoea), *kāsa* (cough), *arśas* (piles), *kṣaya* (consumption) and *kārśya* (emaciation).

Curd of Sheep's Milk

Taste: Sweet.
Vipāka: Sweet.

Notes: (i) It is *abhiṣyandi* (which obstructs the channels of circulation).
(ii) It generally aggravates *doṣas*.
(iii) It produces *durnnāma* (piles), *vātāsra* (gout) and *kapha*.

Curd of Buffalo's Milk

Attributes: Heavy and unctuous.
Vipāka: Sweet.

Specific action: *Vṛṣya* (aphrodisiac) and alleviator of *vāyu* and *pitta*.

Notes:(i) It aggravates *kapha*.
(ii) It vitiates blood.

Curd of Woman's Milk

Attributes: Heavy and ununctuous.
Vipāka: Sweet.
Action: Exceedingly digestive stimulant.
Specific action: Promoter of eye-sight and strength, refreshing and alleviator of all the three *doṣas*.

Curd of Elephant's Milk
Anurasa (Subsidiary taste): Astringent.
Potency: Hot.
Vipāka: Pungent.
Specific action: Alleviates *kapha* and *vāyu*. It increases the quantity of stool.

Note: It suppresses the power of digestion.

Curd of Camel-Milk

Taste: Sour.
Vipāka: Pungent.
Specific action: Purgative and alleviator of *vāyu*.
Therapeutic usage: Cures *udara* (obstinate abdominal diseases including ascites), *kuṣṭha* (obstinate skin diseases including leprosy), *arśas* (piles), *bandha* (constipation) and *krimi* (parasitic infestation).

Note: It is alkaline.

Curd of Mare's Milk

Taste: Sweet.
Attribute: Ununctuous.
Action: Digestiive stimulant.
Specific action: Promotes eye-sight and alleviates *kapha*.

Therapeutic usage: Cures urinary diseases.

Notes:(i) It is *abhiṣyandi* (which obstructs the channels of circulation).
(ii) It aggravates *doṣas* specially *vāyu*.

Among all the above mentioned varieties of curd, the curd prepared from cow's milk is the best and useful.

Gālita Dadhi (Curd of which the Watery Portion is Removed by Filtering)

Taste: Sweet.
Attributes: Heavy and exceedingly unctuous.
Specific action: Promotes strength, nourishment and appetite, and alleviates *vāyu*.

Notes:(i) It aggravates *kapha*.
(ii) It does not aggravate *pitta* in excess.

Curd of Boiled Milk

Attribute: Ununctuous.
Specific action: Promotes all the *dhātus* (tissue elements), *agni* (power of digestion), *bala* (strength) and appetite, and alleviates *pitta* and *vāyu*.

Note: It is exceedingly useful.

Chacchikā or Asāra Dadhi (Curd which is Free from Fat)

Taste: Astringent.
Attribute: Light.
Action: *Dīpana* (digestive stimulant).
Specific action: Constipative and appetiser.
Therapeutic usage: Cures *grahaṇī* (sprue syndrome).

Notes:(i) It is *viṣṭambhi* (which produces wind in the abdomen).
(ii) It aggravates *vāyu*.

Mixed Curd

Curd added with sugar is very useful. It cures *tṛṣṇā* (morbid thirst), *dāha* (burning syndrome), vitiation of blood and alleviates *pitta*.

Curd added with *guḍa* (jaggery) is heavy.

It is aphrodisiac, nourishing, refreshing and alleviator of *vāyu*.

Curd in Different Seasons

Generally, intake of curd is not useful in spring, autumn, summer and rainy season. On the other hand, in *hemanta* (early winter) and *śiśira* (late winter) intake of curd is beneficial.

Use of Curd in Particular Diseases

For a patient suffering from the following diseases intake of curd during day time is useful:

Mūtra kṛcchra (dysuria), *aruci* (anorexia), *śītāṅga* (feeling of cold in the body), *viṣama jvara* (irregular fever), *atisāra* (diarrhoea) and *pratiśyāya* (cold).

Curd should not be taken at night.

Curd when mixed with water and ghee is useful.

Dadhyuttara or Sara (Upper Layer of the Curd which is Dense and Unctuous)

Taste: Sour.
Attribute: Heavy.
Specific action: Laxative, aphrodisiac and alleviator of *vāyu*.
It cleanses urinary bladder.

Notes: (i) It suppresses the power of digestion.
(ii) It aggravates *pitta* and *kapha*.

Mastu (Watery Portion of the Curd)

Attribute: Light.
Specific action: Promotes strength and appetite for food and alleviates *kapha* and *vāyu*.
It is refreshing, instant laxative and giver of happiness.

Therapeutic usage: Cures *klama* (mental fatigue) and *tṛṣṇā* (morbid thirst).

Notes: (i) It is not aphrodisiac.
(ii) It cleanses the *srotas* (channels of circulation).

Ghola, Mathita, Udaśvit and Takra (Butter-milk)

Varieties of Butter-milk

Butter-milk which contains *rasa* (cream) and to which water is not added is called *ghola*.

Butter-milk from which cream is removed is called *mathita*.

When equal quantity of water is added and churned then it is called *śveta*.

When half the quantity of water is added and churned then it is known as *udaśvit*.

When one-fourth quantity of water is added and churned then it is called *takra*. According to some others, in *takra* half the quantity of water is added.

Takra

Taste: Sweet, sour and astringent.
Attributes: Light and ununctuous.
Potency: Hot.
Action: *Dīpana* (digestive stimulant).
Specific action: Constipative, strength promoting, refreshing and alleviator of *vāyu* as well as *kapha*.
Therapeutic usage: Cures *śotha* (oedema), *gara*, (poisoning), *chardi* (vomiting), *praseka* (salivation), *viṣama jvara* (irregular fever), *pāṇḍu* (anemia), *medas* (fat), *grahaṇī* (sprue syndrome), *arśas* (piles), *mūtra graha* (anuria), *bhagandara* (fistula-in-ano), *meha* (obstinate urinary disorders including diabetes), *gulma* (phantom tumour), *atīsāra* (diarrhoea), *śūla* (colic pain), *plīhan* (splenic disorders), *krimi* (parasitic infestation), *śvitra kuṣṭha* (leucoderma), *kuṣṭha* (obstinate skin diseases including leprosy), *kapha vyādhi* (diseases caused by the vitiation of *kapha*), *tṛṣṇā* (morbid thirst), *udara* (obstinate abdominal diseases including ascites) and *apacī* (cervical adenitis).

Contra-indications of Takra

Intake of *takra* (butter-milk) is not useful in summer and autumn seasons. It should also never be taken by a patient who is suffering from *daurbalya* (weakness), *śrama* (physical fatigue), *mūrcchā* (fainting), *pittāsra* or *rakta pitta* (a disease characterised by bleeding from different parts of the body), *mada* (alcoholism) and *śoṣa* (consumption).

Takra (butter-milk) is like an ambrosia in winter, in *grahaṇī* (sprue syndrome), *arśas* (piles), diseases caused by *kapha* and *vāyu*, *srota nirodha* (obstruction to the channels of circulation) and *mandāgni* (suppression of the power of digestion).

Property of Different Types of Takra

Takra (butter-milk) having sweet taste alleviates *vāyu* and *pitta* and aggravates *kapha*.

Takra (butter-milk) having sour taste alleviates *vāyu* and aggravates *rakta* (blood) as well as *pitta*.

Combination with Takra

If *vāyu* is aggravated, sour variety of butter-milk mixed with *saindhava* (rock-salt) should be taken.

If there is aggravation of *pitta*, then sweet variety of butter-milk mixed with sugar should be taken.

If there is aggravation of *kapha*, then ununctuous type of butter-milk mixed with *vyoṣa (suṇṭhī, pippalī* and *marica)* and alkalies should be taken.

Properties of Different Types of Takra

Takra (Butter-milk) from which Fat is completely removed

Attribute: Light.

It is wholesome.

Takra from which less Quantity of Fat is Removed

Attributes: Heavy.
Specific action: Aphrodisiac and alleviator of *kapha*.

Takra from which Fat is Completely Removed

Attributes: Heavy and *sāndra* (dense).
Specific action: Nourishing.

Note: It aggravates *kapha*.

The properties of different eight types of curd *(dadhi)* prepared from different types of milk are shared by the butter-milk prepared out of them.

WATER

Potency: Cold.
Specific action: Cardiac tonic and alleviator of *pitta*.
Therapeutic usage: Cures *viṣa* (poisoning), *bhrama* (giddiness), *dāha* (burning sensation), *ajīrṇa* (indigestion), *śrama* (exhaustion), *chardi* (vomiting), *mada* (intoxication), *mūrcchā* (fainting) and *madātyaya* (alcoholism).

Contra-indications of Cold Water

Cold water should not be used in the following diseases and conditions:

- *stimita koṣṭha* (absence of peristaltic movement in the intestine);
- *gala roga* (throat diseases);
- *nava jvara* (first stage of fever);
- *grahaṇī* (sprue syndrome);
- *pīnasa* (rhinitis);
- *ādhmāna* (flatulence);
- *hikkā* (hiccup);
- *gulma* (phantom tumour);
- *vidradhi* (abscess);

- *kāsa* (cough)
- *meha* (obstinate urinary disorders including diabetes);
- *aruci* (anorexia);
- *śvāsa* (dyspnoea);
- *pāṇḍu* (anemia);
- *vātāmaya* (diseases caused by vitiated *vāyu*);
- *pārśva śūla* (colic pain in the side of the chest);
- immediately after the intake of *sneha* (oil, ghee, etc.); and
- after the administration of *śodhana* (elimination) therapy (purgation, emesis, etc.).

Varieties of Over-ground Water

(Over-ground) water is of four types, viz,

I. *Divya* (rain-water collected before falling on the ground).
II. *Tuṣāraja* (water collected from dew and frost).
III. *Dhāra* (rain-water after it falls on the ground).
IV. *Kārahaima* (water from hailstone and snow).

Of them, *divya* type of water is the best because of its lightness. It is again of two types as follows:

Two varieties of Ākāśajala (Rain Water)

The *divya* or *ākāśa* (rain) type of water is of two types, namely, *gāṅga* (which is derived from the Ganges) and *samudraja* (which is derived from the sea).

Gāṅga water is better than *samudraja.*

The *sāmudra* type of water which rains in the month of *āśvina* (September-October), is similar to *gāṅga* type of water in its properties.

Test for Gāṅga Water

If to the water, contained in a golden, silver or new earthen pot, boiled *śāli* rice is kept soaked, and it does not become *kledi* (undergo deterioration) and retains its natural colour, then this water is to be determined as *Gāṅga*.

This water alleviates all the three *doṣas* and cures *viṣa* (poisoning).

Properties of Gāṅga Water

It alleviates all the three *doṣas*, viz., *vāyu, pitta* and *kapha*.

Sāmudra Water

It is alkaline and mixed with *lavaṇa* (salt).
It reduces *śukra* (semen), *dṛṣṭi* (eye-sight) and *bala* (strength).

Divya Jala (Rain Water)

Taste: It has no manifested taste.
Attribute: Light.
Potency: *Saumya* (cold).
Specific action: Rejuvenating, *balya* (strength promoting), *jīvana* (life-giving), *tarpaṇa* (refreshing), giver of consolation and happiness, promoter of intellect in excess and alleviator of all the three *doṣas*.
Therapeutic usage: Cures *tṛṣā* (morbid thirst), *mūrcchā* (fainting), *tandrā* (drowsiness), *dāha* (burning syndrome), *klama* (mental fatigue), *mahā nidrā* (excessive sleep) and *śrama* (exhaustion).

Bhauma Jala (Ground Water)

Divya type of water (rain water) when falls on the ground is called *Bhauma jala* (ground water).

Attributes of Different Types of Water

When *divya* type of water (rain water) is not available then after ascertaining the advantages and disadvantages of the different types of the ground-water one should use them.

Kaupa Jala (Well-Water)

Attribute: Light.
Action: Digestive stimulant.
Specific action : Alleviates *kapha*.

Notes: (i) It is *kṣāra* (alkaline).
(ii) It aggravates *pitta*.

Tāḍāga Jala (Pond-Water)

Taste: Sweet and astringent.
Vipāka: Pungent.

Note: It aggravates *vāyu*.

Vāpya Jala (Water of Small Pond)

Taste: Pungent.
Specific action: Alleviates *vāyu* and *kapha*.

Notes: (i) It is alkaline.
(ii) It aggravates *pitta*.

Nairjhara Jala (Spring-Water)

Attribute: Light.
Action: *Dīpana* (digestive stimulant).
Specific action: Cardiac tonic, *lekhana* (depleting) and alleviator of *kapha*.

Hrāda Jala (Lake-Water)

Attribute: Light.
Action: Exceedingly digestive stimulant.
Specific action: Alleviates *pitta*.

Note: It is *avidāhi* (which does not cause burning sensation).

Cauḍya Jala (Water of a Big Well)

Taste: Sweet.
Attribute: Unctuous.
Action: Stimulant of digestive power.

Note: It does not aggravate *kapha*.

Nādeya Jala (River-Water)

Attributes: Light and unuctuous.
Action: Digestive stimulant.
Specific action: *Lekhana* (depleting).

Note: It aggravates *vāyu*.

Sārasa Jala (Water of Tank)

Taste: Sweet and astringent.
Attribute: Light.
Specific action: Strength promoting.
Therapeutic usage: Cures *tṛṣṇā* (morbid thirst).

Kaidāra Jala (Water of Field)

Attribute: Heavy.
Vipāka: Sweet.

Notes: (i) It is *abhiṣyandi* (which obstructs the channels of circulation).
(ii) It aggravates *doṣas*.

Pālvala Jala (Water of Small Pond)

This water is similar to *kāntāra* (water of field) in properties. Specifically, it aggravates all the *doṣas*.

Tauṣāra Jala (Water from Dew and Frost)

Attribute: Ununctuous.
Potency: Cold.
Specific action : Alleviates *pitta* and *kapha*.

Note: It aggravates *vāyu*.

Rain-Water

Divya (rain) water before it falls on the earth viz., collected directly from the sky alleviates all the *doṣas*.

Kāra Jala (Water from Hail-Stone)

Attributes: Heavy, ununctuous and *viśada* (non-slimy).
Potency: Cold.
Specific action: Alleviates *kapha* and *vāyu*.

Haima Jala (Water from Snow)

Attribute: Comparatively heavy.
Potency: Cold.
Specific action: Alleviates *pitta*.

Note: It aggravates *vāyu*.

Candrakānta Jala (Water Collected with the help of a Moon-Stone)

Attributes: Light and ununctuous.
Specific action: Alleviates *pitta*.
Therapeutic usage: Cures *viṣa* (poisoning) and *asra* (vitiation of blood).

Nārikela Jala (Coconut Water)

Taste: Sweet.
Attributes: Light and unctuous.
Potency: Cold.
Action: Digestive stimulant.
Specific action: Aphrodisiac, cardiac tonic and alleviates *pitta*.
Therapeutic usage: Cures *pipāsā* (morbid thirst). It cleanses *basti* (urinary bladder).

Haṃsodaka

Definition: Water which is exposed to the sun's rays during the day time and to the moon's rays at night is called *haṃsodaka*.
Attributes: Light and unctuous.
Potency: Cold.
Specific action: *Rasāyana* (rejuvenating), *balya* (strength promoting),

medhya ((intellect promoting) and alleviator of all the three *doṣas* namely, *vāyu, pitta* and *kapha*.

Notes: (i) It is like *āntarikṣa jala* (water collected directly from the sky).
(ii) It is free from defects.
(iii) It is *anabhiṣyandi* (which does not obstruct the channels of circulation).
(iv) It is like an ambrosia.

Water in Different Seasons

During rainy season, *divya* (water collected directly from the sky) or *audbhida* (water that comes out by piercing the earth) type of water is useful.

During autumn, clean water which is impregnated with the rays of *Agastya* (star Canopus) and has become free from the poison is useful.

In *hemanta* (early winter), *sārasa* (water of big tank) or *tāḍāga* (water of pond) is useful.

In spring and summer seasons, water of well, small pond and spring is useful.

In the rainy season, water from *cauṇḍya* (big-well) and all other types of water which are *aviṣṭambhi* (do not aggravate *vāyu*) are useful.

Attributes of River-Water

Rivers flowing with strong current and having clean water are light. Rivers flowing with slow current, full of dirt and associated with *śaivāla* (moss) are heavy. Water from rivers which originate from the Himalayas and pass through stones is wholesome.

Water from the Gaṅgā, Śatadru, Sarayū and Yamunā has excellent properties.

Water of these rivers is clean and sacred. It alleviates *vāyu* and *kapha* and slightly aggravates *pitta*.

The rivers whose source is the Malaya mountain, are of strong current, light and useful.

The rivers like Vṛta mālā and Tāmraparṇī carry clean water.

The rivers whose water is stable and other rivers originating from these produce *ślīpada* (filariasis), *apacī* (cervical adenitis), *śotha* (oedema), diseases of feet, head, throat and neck, *arbuda* (tumour) and *krimi* (parasitic infestation).

The rivers like Veṇī, Godāvarī, etc., whose source is the Sahya mountain carry water which usually causes *kuṣṭha* (obstinate skin diseases including leprosy). Water of some of these rivers alleviates *vāyu* and *kapha*.

The rivers like Śiprā, Revā, etc., whose source is the Vindhyācala mountain carry water which produces *pāṇḍu* (anemia) and *kuṣṭha* (obstinate skin diseases including leprosy.

The rivers like Carmaṇvatī, whose source is the Pāriyātra mountain, are of two types:

(i) *Rivers which are originating from taḍāga (pond)*: Water of these rivers alleviates all the three *doṣas* and reduces strength.
(ii) *Rivers which are originated from darī (caves)*: Water of these rivers produces *kuṣṭha* (obstinate skin diseases including leprosy), *kaṇḍu* (itches), *kapha, ślīpada* (filariasis) and *agni* (power of digestion).

Water of other rivers which flow towards the east causes *gudaja* (piles). The rivers originating from deserts carry water which has following properties:

Taste: Sweet.
Attribute: Light.
Action: Excessively stimulant of digestion.
Specific action: Strength promoting.

The rivers Gomatī, Narmadā, etc., which flow towards the sea in the west carry water which has following properties:

Specific action: Strength promoting and alleviator of *pitta* and *kapha*.
Therapeutic usage: Cures *vātāsra* (gout) and *kaṇḍū* (itching).

The rivers which flow towards the sea in the south carry water, which has following properties:

Specific action: Strength promoting and alleviator of *pitta*.

Note: It aggravates *kapha* and *vāyu*.

The rivers which flow towards the sea in the east are of slow current and their water is heavy.

Sea-Water

It reduces strength and virility.
It aggravates all the three *doṣas*.

Time of Collection

All types of water available on the ground should be collected early in the morning because during this time, they are clean and cold par excellence.

Time of Taking Water

Water taken before taking food causes *kārśya* (emaciation) and *mandāgni* (suppression of the power of digestion). When it is taken during eating, it stimulates the power of digestion, and this is the best. If it is taken after the meal, then it causes *sthaulya* (adiposity) and aggravation of *kapha*.

Different Modes of Taking Water

Water is the life of all living beings and the entire world is pervaded by water. Therefore, intake of water should never be prohibited by the wise persons, in spite of strong contra-indications.

In some cases, hot water should be taken, in some cases cold water should be taken, and in some other cases cold water after boiling or water boiled by adding some drugs should be taken. However, it should never be prohibited.

Water of another place should not be taken. In *ajīrṇa* (indigestion) associated with *āma* (first stage) boiled water and in *pakva* (later) state of *ajīrṇa* (indigestion), clean water should be taken.

It there is *vidagdha* (incomplete digestion) state of food and if the person is thirsty, then he should take cold water. By this, *vidāha* (burning sensation) gets cured and residual food gets digested.

Properties of Ānūpa Jala, etc.

Ānūpa Jala (Water found in Marshy Areas)

This type of water is *abhiṣyandi* (which obstructs the channels of circulation), despicable and aggravator of *doṣas*.

Jāṅgala Jala (Water found in Arid Areas)

This type of water stimulates the power of digestion and alleviates all the *doṣas*.

Sādhāraṇa Jala (Water found in the Land of Moderate Nature)

Taste: Sweet.
Attribute: Light.
Potency: Cold.
Therapeutic usage: Cures *tṛṣṇā* (morbid thirst).

Note: It causes exhileration.

Prohibited Water

In rainy season, a person who takes bath in fresh rain water, who takes fresh water (water which is collected from the ground immediately after rain) and water which is mixed or polluted with leaves, etc., suffers from external and internal diseases.

Polluted Water

Water which is *kaluṣa* (dirty or unclean), covered with lotus leaves, moss, grass, etc., which has putrid smell, etc., and which is not exposed to the rays of sun as well as moon is to be considered as polluted water.

This polluted water vitiates all the three *doṣas*.

Water collected from unseasonal rain should also not be taken.

Method for Removing Pollution

Polluted water should be boiled and exposed to the sun rays. In this water hot piece of iron, *sūrya maṇi*, sand pebbles, etc. should be immersed. Then this should be impregnated with *karpūra, pura (guggulu)*, *punnāga, pāṭalā*, etc. This clean water should be cooled by adding *kanaka* (gold), *muktā* (pearl), etc. This cold water never aggravates *doṣas* (is not harmful).

Boiled Water

The water which is boiled, free from foam and movement, and clear possesses the following properties:

Attribute: Light.
Action: *Dīpana* (digestive stimulant) and *pācana* (carminative).
Specific action: Alleviates all the *doṣas* viz., *vāyu, pitta* and *kapha*.

Hot Water

Attribute: Light.
Action: Stimulates the power of digestion.
Specific action: Alleviates *vāyu* and *kapha*.
Therapeutic usage: Cures *pārśva ruk* (pain in the sides of the chest), *pīnasa* (rhinitis), *ādhmāna* (flatulence) and *hikkā* (hiccup).

Note: It cleanses *basti* (urinary tract).

Water Reduced to 3/4th After Boiling

It alleviates *vāyu*

Water Reduced to Half After Boiling

It alleviates *pitta*.

Note: It is useful in *hemanta* (early winter), *śiśira* (late winter), *varṣ* (rainy season) and spring seasons.

Water Reduced to ¼th After Boiling

Attribute: Light.
Action: Stimulates the power of digestion.

Specific action: Constipative and alleviator of *kapha*.

Note: It is useful in summer and autumn.

Intake of Hot Water at Night

When hot water is taken at night, it cleans the adhesion of *kapha*, helps in the elimination of *vāyu* and removes indigestion immediately.

Cold Water After Boiling

Attribute: Light.
Specific action: Alleviates all the three *doṣas*.

Notes:(i) This water is always wholesome.
(ii) This water is harmful if stale (kept overnight) and becomes full of impurities (or polluted).

If the water is boiled during the day time and kept over night, it becomes heavy. Similarly, if water is boiled at night and taken next day, it excessively aggravates all the *doṣas*.

Time Taken for the Digestion of Water

Unboiled water gets digested in one *yāma* (three hours). The water which is boiled and cooled gets digested in half *yāma* (one and half hour). The water which is boiled and warm takes one *muhūrta* (forty eight minutes) for digestion. These are the three different times for the digestion of water.

Taking Less of Water

In *arocaka* (anorexia), *pratiśyāya* (coryza), *praseka* (salivation), *śvayathu* (oedema), *kṣaya* (consumption), *mandāgni* (suppression of the power of digestion), *udara* (obstinate abdominal diseases including ascites), *kuṣṭha* (obstinate skin diseases including leprosy), *jvara* (fever), *netrāmaya* (eye-diseases), *vraṇa* (ulcer) and *madhumeha* (diabetes mellitus), one should take less quantity of water.

Importance of Water

A thirsty person (if not given water) becomes unconscious and succumbs to death. Therefore, with all care, water should not be prohibited.

In *mūrcchā* (fainting), vitiation of *pitta, uṣṇa* (excessive hot feeling), *dāha* (burning sensation), *viṣa* (poisoning) and vitiation of blood cold water should be given.

Prohibition of Warm Water

In *śrama* (exhaustion), *klama* (mental fatigue), *parikṣepa* (convulsions), *tamaka śvāsa* (a type of bronchial asthma), *kṣut* (hunger) and *ūrdhvaga rakta pitta* (bleeding through upper parts of the body), intake of hot water should be avoided.

Prohibition of Cold Water

In *pārśva śūla* (pain in the sides of the chest), *pratiśyāya* (coryza), *vāta roga* (diseases caused by the vitiatiton of *vāyu*), *gala graha* (obstruction in the throat), *ādhmāna* (flatulence), *timira* (cataract), *koṣṭha* (constipation), *sadyaḥ śūla* (freshly occurring colic pain), *nava jvara* (beginning stage of fever), *hikkā* (hiccup) and *sneha pāna* (immediately after oleation therapy), cold water should be avoided.

Taking the Excess of Water

If water is taken in excess, it suppresses the power of digestion. If water is not taken at all, it produces several ailments. Therefore, with a view to promoting the power of digestion, one should take water very frequently in small quantities.

These items are often used in the Specialised Massage Therapy as food and drinks. For the preparation of medicated oils and such other recipes, these ingredients are commonly used. The physician should be well acquainted with the therapeutic properties of these ingredients as described in Ayurveda. This will enable him to select the most appropriate ingredient for successful administration of Massage Therapy.

ABBREVIATIONS USED FOR PARTS OF PLANTS IN RECIPES OF APPENDIX-III

1.	Androcium	Adr.
2.	Anther	Atr.
3.	Aril	Ar.
4.	Bulb	Bl.
5.	Dry Fruit	Dr. Fr.
6.	Dry Seed	Dr. Sd.
7.	Exudate	Exd.
8.	Endosperm *(Bīja Majjā)*	Enm.
9.	Flower	Fl.
10.	Fruit	Fr.
11.	Fruit Rind	Fr. R.
12.	Fruit Pulp *(Phala Majjā)*	Fr. P.
13.	Gall	Gl.
14.	Heart Wood	Ht. Wd.
15.	Inflorescence	Ifl.
16.	Leaf	Lf.
17.	Latex	L.
18.	Oil	Ol.
19.	Plant (Whole)	Pl.
20.	Root	Rt.
21.	Root Bark	Rt. Bk.
22.	Root Tuber	Rt. Tr.
23.	Rhizome	Rz.
24.	Seed	Sd.
25.	Stem	St.
26.	Stem Bark	St. Bk.
27.	Stem Tuber	St. Tr.
28.	Style & Stigma	Stl./Stg.
29.	Substitute Root	Sub. Rt.

APPENDIX-III

PHARMACEUTICAL PROCESS FOR MANUFACTURING MEDICATED OIL AND RECIPES[1]

Medicated Oils are preparations in which oil is boiled with prescribed decoctions and pastes of drugs according to the prescribed procedure. This process ensures absorption of the active therapeutic properties of the ingredients used. Mostly oil soluble fractions of these ingredients are collected through this process. Some fine particles of these ingredients remain suspended in the medicated oil even after filteration and the theraeutic properties of these insoluble fractions are also available for use through these medicated oils. According to Ayurveda, oil has the specific property to absorb the therapeutically useful fractions of drugs.

General Method of Preparation

Generally three important types of ingredients are used in the preparation of medicated oil which are as follows:

(a) Oil which is used as media;
(b) Paste of drugs; and
(c) Liquids which may be one or more in number, like decoction, juice, milk, etc.

Unless otherwise mentioned in the text, the paste is one fourth of the quantity of the oil and the liquid is four times of the quantity of the oil. In other words, paste is one part, the oil is four parts and the liquid(s) are sixteen parts. According to this ratio, generally many of the medicated oils are prepared. In addition, the physician should keep in view the following points:

(a) If, in the recipe, no liquid is mentioned, then four parts of water is used in the preparation.

----

1. Based on the Ayurvedic Formulary of India, Part I, Published by Ministry of Health & F.W., New Delhi (1st ed.), 1978.

(b) If the liquid is either decoction or juice of a plant, then the paste should be one-sixth and one-eighth respectively of the quantity of the oil.
(c) Where the number of the liquids is four or less than four, then each of the liquids has to be taken four times the weight of the oil.
(d) Where the liquids are more than four in number, then each liquid has to be equal in weight to the oil.
(e) If, in a preparation, no paste is prescribed, then the drugs prescribed for the purpose of decoction may be used as paste.

The paste and the liquid are mixed together, and the oil is then added, boiled and stirred well continuously so that the paste is not allowed to adhere to the bottom of the vessel. Some times, the liquids are required to be added one after the other and the process of boiling is continued till the liquids added earlier are completely evaporated (the moisture part of it).

When the moisture from all the liquids is evaporated, then the moisture part of the paste begins to evaporate. At this stage, the preparation has to be carefully examined more often to ensure that the paste does not get charred and stick to the bottom of the vessel. A small portion of the paste is taken out with the help of the ladle and examined from time to time to ascertain the condition and the stage of the cooking (*pāka*).

There are three different stages of cooking (*pāka*) as follows:

(a) Mild cooking (*Mṛdu pāka*);
(b) Moderate cooking (*Madhyama pāka*); and
(c) Over cooking (*Khara pāka*).

In mild-cooking stage, the paste is waxy when rolled between two fingers and the paste rolls like a paste of lac without sticking to the fingers. In moderate stage of cooking, the paste, when rolled, is harder and when it is placed over the flame of the fire, it burns without any cracking noise. A further application of heat leads to over-cooking. If out of ignorance or carelessness, further heat is applied, then the oil gets burnt and in ayurvedic parlance, it is called *dagdha pāka* which renders the medicated oil absolutely useless of therapeutic purpose. When the oil reached the correct sage of cooking, then froth comes out at the surface and at this stage the physician should repeatedly examine the paste.

When the medicated oil is prescribed to be prepared by adding several liquids, like decoction, juice, milk, meat soup, vinegar and butter-milk, the period of cooking with various liquids should be as follows:

(a) Decoction, vinegar and butter-milk, etc.	5 days in each.
(b) Juice	3 days
(c) Milk	2 days
(d) Meat soup	1 day

If sugar is described as one of the ingredients in the recipe, then it is to be added after the final product has cooled down. If salts and alkali preparations are mentioned as ingredients of a medicated oil, then these are to be added to the finished product and then strained.

Adding Perfumes

If to a recipe of medicated oil, perfumes or aromatic substances are to be added for flavour, then the powders or solutions of these ingredients are placed over a strainer and the medicated oil, when luke-warm, is poured over it. This enables the oil to be impregnated with the aroma.

Utility of Different Types of Cooking

The medicated oil prepared by mild cooking is useful for inhalation therapy. The medicated oil prepared by moderate cooking is useful for massage of the body, medicated enema and taking internally. The over-cooked medicated oil is useful for massage, specially for the massage of the head.

Vessels for Cooking

Copper vessel is very useful for cooking the medicated oil. But if sour things like vinegar and butter-milk or yoghurt are to be used for cooking, then stainless steel vessel should be used for cooking. The capacity of the vessel should be minimum double the volume of the oil and liquids taken together. This will prevent the overflowing of the oil during the process of cooking. The ladle or the stirrer should be made of either copper or stainless steel and it should have a square and flat surface at the bottom to facilitate stirring. It should have a wooden handle at the distal end to facilitate holding it without difficulty during the process.

Now a days, cooking of medicated oils is done in vessels having double walls with space in between for the hot steam to pass. This is more hygienic and it prevents charring of the paste at the bottom of the vessel.

Fuel

For the cooking of some of the medicated oils, charcoals of different types wood are prescribed in ayurvedic classics. In general practice, coal, charcoal, gas (liquid patroleum gas) and steam are used for the preparation of the oil. Whatever the fuel may be, in the beginning and at the end of the process, the heat should be mild and in the middle of the process, gradually strong heat can be applied. Strong heat at the final stage may cause charring of the paste and thus, render the peparation unfit for medical use. It may also cause overflow of the hot oil leading to fire hazzards.

Characteristics

The medicated oil generally possesses the colour, odour and taste of the ingredients which are used in the preparation. They also affect the consistency of the final product. When large quantity of milk is added to the preparation, then the medicated oil becomes thick in consistency because of the butter or ghee content of it. Such preparations get condensed like butter or ghee in winter or when stored in a refrigerator.

Preservation

Medicated oils are to be stored in glass or good quality polythene containers. Such medicated oils stored properly, retain their potency for about sixteen months for the purpose of internal use. For massage, these preparations cooked properly and stored in proper containers can be used for about five years, after manufacture.

Method of Use

Medicated oils are generally used for massage of the body and head. These are also used for inhalation therapy, medicated enema and external application. Medicated oils are also used internally. In Ayurvedic texts, several types of vehicles are prescribed for this purpose. When no such vehicle is specified, then the medicated oil should be taken along with warm milk or warm water. When the oil of *Semecarpus anacardium (bhallātaka)* and such other ingredients are included in the preparation, then the use of warm vehicle is prohibited.

Recipes of some of the commonly used medicated oils are described hereafter.

ASANAVBILVĀDI TAILA

(Sahasrayoga, Tailaprakaraṇa; 45)

1.	Asana	(Ht. Wd.)	192 g.
2.	Bilva	(Rt.)	192 g.
3.	Balā	(Rt.)	192 g.
4.	Amṛtā (guḍūcī)	(St.)	192 g.
5.	Water for decoction		12.288 l.
	reduced to		3.072 l.
6.	Taila		768 ml.
7.	Madhuka	(Rt.)	128 g.
8.	Nāgaraka	(Rz.)	128 g.
9.	Harītakī	(Fr. P.)	128 g.
10.	Bibhītaka	(Fr. P.)	128 g.
11.	Āmalakī	(Fr. P.)	128 g.
12.	Paya (Cow's milk)		

Usage:
Used externally for massage.
Important therapeutic use:
Diseases of eyes, ears and head.

KANAKA TAILA

(Bhaiṣajyaratnāvalī, Kṣudrarogādhikāra; 59)

1.	Madhuka (yaṣṭī madhu)	(Rt.)	768 g.

2.	Water for decoction reduced to		3.072 l. 768 ml.
3.	Taila		192 ml.
4.	Priyaṅgu	(Fl.)	32 g.
5.	Manjīṣṭhā	(St.)	32 g.
6.	Candana (śveta candana)	(Ht. Wd.)	32 g.
7.	Utpala (puṣpa)	(Fl.)	32 g.
8.	Kesara (nāga keśara)	(Fl.)	32 g.

Usage:
Used externally for *nasya* and massage.
Important therapeutic use:
Discoloration of the skin.

KAYYONNYĀDI TAILA

(Sahasrayoga, Tailaprakaraṇa; 48)

1.	Kayyonni (bhṛṅga rāja) rasa	(Pl.)	1.024 l.
2.	Ciṭṭamṛtu (guḍūcī) rasa	(St.)	1.024 l.
3.	Nelli (āmalakī rasa)	(Fr. P.)	1.024 l.
4.	Taila		768 ml.
5.	Payas (gokṣīra)		768 g.
6.	Madhuka (yaṣṭī madhu)	(Rt.)	48 g.
7.	Añjana (rasāñjana) (dārvī ghana)		48 g.

Usage:
Used externally for head-massage.
Important therapeutic use:
Diseases of head, hair, eyes and teeth.

KĀRPĀSĀSTHYĀDI TAILA

(Sahasrayoga, Tailaprakaraṇa, 11.)

1.	Kārpāsāsthi (kārppāsa bīja)	(Enm.)	768 g.
2.	Balā	(Rt.)	768 g.
3.	Māṣa	(Sd.)	768 g.
4.	Kulattha	(Sd.)	768 g.

5.	Water for decoction		12.288 l.
	reduced to		3.072 l.
6.	Deva dāru	(Ht. Wd.)	128 g.
7.	Balā	(Rt.)	128 g.
8.	Rāsnā	(Rt.)	128 g.
9.	Kuṣṭha	(Rt.)	128 g.
10.	Sarṣapa	(Sd.)	128 g.
11.	Nāgara	(Rz.)	128 g.
12.	Śatāhvā	(Fl.)	128 g.
13.	Pippalimūla	(Rt.)	128 g.
14.	Cavya	(St.)	128 g.
15.	Śigru (tvak)	(St. Bk.)	128 g.
16.	Punarnavā	(Rt.)	128 g.
17.	Taila		768 ml.
18.	Ajā kṣīra		768 ml.

Special method of preparation:
Kārpāsāsthi, kulattha, and *maṣa* are tied in a bundle and immersed in the vessel containing *balāmūla* and water. *Balākaṣāya* (decoction of *balā*) is then prepared.
Usage: Used externally for massage.
Important Therapeutic use: Hemiplegia, facial paralysis, frozen shoulders and other nervous disorders.

KUṄKUMĀDI TAILA

(Yogaratnākara, Kṣudrarogādhikāra; page 740)

1.	Kuṅkuma	(Stl./Stg.)	12 g.
2.	Candana (śveta candana)	(Ht. Wd.)	12 g.
3.	Lodhra	(St. Bk.)	12 g.
4.	Pataṅga	(Fl.)	12 g.
5.	Rakta candana	(Ht. Wd.)	12 g.
6.	Mālīyaka (aguru)	(Ht. Wd.)	12 g.
7.	Uśīra	(Rt.)	12 g.
8.	Mañjiṣṭhā	(St.)	12 g.
9.	Madhu yaṣṭī	(Rt.)	12 g.
10.	Patra (teja patra)	(Lf.)	12 g.
11.	Padmaka	(Ht. Wd.)	12 g.
12.	Padma (kamala)	(Fl.)	12 g.

13. Kuṣṭha	(Rt.)	12 g.
14. Gorocanā		12 g.
15. Niśā (haridrā)	(Rz.)	12 g.
16. Lākṣā	(Exd.)	12 g.
17. Dāru haridrā	(St.)	12 g.
18. Gairika		12 g.
19. Nāga keśara	(Fl.)	12 g.
20. Palāśa kusuma	(Fl.)	12 g.
21. Priyaṅgu	(Fl.)	12 g.
22. Vaṭāṅkura	(Lf.)	12 g.
23. Mālatī	(Fl.)	12 g.
24. Madhūcchiṣṭa		12 g.
25. Sarṣapa	(Sd.)	12 g.
26. Surabhi (rāsnā)	(Rt.)	12 g.
27. Vacā	(Rz.)	12 g.
28. Paya (kṣīra)		6.144 l.
29. Taila		1.536 l.

Usage:
Used externally for massage.
Important therapeutic use: Skin diseases.

KUṢṬHARĀKṢASA TAILA

(Bhaiṣajyaratnāvalī, Kuṣṭhādhikāra; 164-165 ½)

1. Sūtaka (pārada)		12 g.
2. Gandhaka		12 g.
3. Kuṣṭha	(Rt.)	12 g.
4. Saptaparṇa (tvak)	(St. Bk.)	12 g.
5. Citraka	(Rt.)	12 g.
6. Sindūra		12 g.
7. Rasona	(Bl.)	12 g.
8. Haritāla		12 g.
9. Avalgujā (bākucī)	(Sd.)	12 g.
10. Āragvadha bīja	(Sd.)	12 g.
11. Jīrṇa tāmra (tāmra bhasma)		12 g.
12. Manaḥśilā		12 g.
13. Kaṭu taila (sarṣapa taila)		384 ml.

Special method of preparation:

Powders of drugs 1 to 8 are mixed in taila and

exposed to sun's rays for a week.
Usage:
Used externally for massage.
Important therapeutic use: Obstinate skin diseases.

KOṬṬAMCUKKĀDDI TAILA

(Sahasrayoga, Tailaprakaraṇa; 12)

1.	Koṭṭam (kuṣṭha)	(Rt.)	96 g.
2.	Cukku (nāgara)	(Rz.)	96 g.
3.	Vayambu (vacā)	(Rz.)	96 g.
4.	Śigru (tvak)	(St. Bk.)	96 g.
5.	Laśuna	(Bl.)	96 g.
6.	Kārtoṭṭi (mūtla)	(Rt.)	96 g.
7.	Devadruma	(Ht. Wd.)	96 g.
8.	Siddhārtha (sarṣapa)	(Sd.)	96 g.
9.	Suvahā (rāsnā)	(Rt./Lf.)	96 g.
10.	Tilaja (tila taila)		768 ml.
11.	Dadhi		768 g.
12.	Ciñcā (patra) rasa	(Lf.)	3.072 l.

Usage:
Used externally for massage.
Important therapeutic use: Rheumatism, arthritis and gout.

KṢĪRABALĀ TAILA

(Aṣṭāṅgahṛdaya, Vātaraktacikitsā, Adhyāya 22; 44 ½)

1.	Balā kaṣāya	(Rt.)	16 parts
2.	Balā kalka	(Rt.)	1 part
3.	Taila		4 parts
4.	Kṣīra		4 parts

Usage: Used externally for massage.
Important therapeutic use: Nervous disorders.

CANDANĀDI TAILA

(Yogaratnākara, Rājayakṣmācikitsā; page 325)

1.	Candana (śveta candana)	(Ht. Wd.)	96 g.

2.	Ambu (hrībera)	(Rt.)	96 g.
3.	Nakha		96 g.
4.	Rātrī (haridrā)	(Rz.)	96 g.
5.	Yaṣṭi (yaṣṭīmadhu)	(Rt.)	96 g.
6.	Śaileya	(Pl.)	96 g.
7.	Padmaka	(Ht. Wd.)	96 g.
8.	Mañjiṣṭhā	(St.)	96 g.
9.	Sarala	(Rt.)	96 g.
10.	Dāru (deva dāru)	(Ht. Wd.)	96 g.
11.	Śaṭī	(Rz.)	96 g.
12.	Elā	(Sd.)	96 g.
13.	Jātī	(Fl.)	96 g.
14.	Kesara	(Fl.)	96 g.
15.	Patra	(Lf.)	96 g.
16.	Bilva	(St. Bk.)	96 g.
17.	Uśīra	(Rt.)	96 g.
18.	Kaṅkola	(Rz.)	96 g.
19.	Candana (rakta candana)	(Ht. Wd.)	96 g.
20.	Ambuda (mustā)	(Rz.)	96 g.
21.	Haridrā	(Rt.)	96 g.
22.	Dāru haridrā	(St.)	96 g.
23.	Śveta sārivā	(Rt.)	96 g.
24.	Kṛṣṇa sārivā	(Rt.)	96 g.
25.	Tiktā (kaṭukī)	(Rz.)	96 g.
26.	Lavaṅga	(Fl.)	96 g.
27.	Aguru	(Ht. Wd.)	96 g.
28.	Kuṅkuma	(Stl./Stg.)	96 g.
29.	Tvak	(St. Bk.)	96 g.
30.	Reṇu (hareṇu)	(Sd.)	96 g.
31.	Nalikā	(Sub. St. Bk.)	96 g.
32.	Taila		768 ml.
33.	Mastu		3.072 l.
34.	Lākṣārasa		768 ml.

Usage: Used externally for massage.
Important therapeutic use: Chronic fever, burning sensation, bleeding from different parts of body, tuberculosis, epilepsy and psyzophrenia.

CANDANABALĀLĀKṢĀDI TAILA
(Yogaratnākara, Jvarādhikāra; page 205)

1.	Candana (rakta candana)	(Ht. Wd.)	768 g.
2.	Balā mūla	(Rt.)	768 g.
3.	Lākṣā	(Exd.)	768 g.
4.	Lāmajjaka	(Pl.)	768 g.
5.	Water for decoction		12.288 l.
	reduced to		3.072 l.
6.	Taila		1.536 l.
7.	Candana (śveta candana)	(Ht. Wd.)	256 g.
8.	Uśīra	(Rt.)	256 g.
9.	Madhuka	(Rt.)	256 g.
10.	Śatāhvā	(Fl.)	256 g.
11.	Kaṭurohiṇī (kaṭuki)	(Rz.)	256 g.
12.	Deva dāru	(Ht. Wd.)	256 g.
13.	Niśā (Haridrā)	(Rz.)	256 g.
14.	Kuṣṭha	(Rt.)	256 g.
15.	Mañjiṣṭhā	(St.)	256 g.
16.	Aguru	(Ht. Wd.)	256 g.
17.	Bālaka (hrībera)	(Rt.)	256 g.
18.	Aśvagandhā	(Rt.)	256 g.
19.	Balā	(Rt.)	256 g.
20.	Dārvī (dāru haridrā)	(St.)	256 g.
21.	Mūrvā	(Rt.)	256 g.
22.	Mustā	(Rz.)	256 g.
23.	Mūlaka	(Rt.)	256 g.
24.	Elā	(Sd.)	256 g.
25.	Tvak	(St. Bk.)	256 g.
26.	Nāga kusuma (nāga keśara)	(Fl.)	256 g.
27.	Rāsnā	(Rt./Lf.)	256 g.
28.	Lākṣā	(Exd.)	256 g.
29.	Sugandhikā (śaṭī)	(Rz.)	256 g.
30.	Campaka	(Fl.)	256 g.
31.	Pītasāra (asana)	(Ht. Wd.)	256 g.
32.	Sārivā	(Rt.)	256 g.
33.	Sauvarcala		256 g.
34.	Saindhava		256 g.
35.	Kṣīra		3.072 l.

Usage: Used for massage.
Important therapeutic use: Asthma, chronic bronchitis, chronic fever, oedema, anemia, skin diseases and nervous disorders.

CITRAAKĀDI TAILA
(Suśrutasaṃhitā, Bhagandara Cikitsā; 50.50 ½)

1.	Citraka	(Rt.)	16 g.
2.	Arka (mūla)	(Rt.)	16 g.
3.	Trivṛt	(Rt.)	16 g.
4.	Pāṭhā	(Rt.)	16 g.
5.	Malapū (kākodumbara mūla tvak)	(Rt. Bk.)	16 g.
6.	Hayamāraka (karavīra mūla tvak)	(Rt. Bk.)	16 g.
7.	Sudhā (snuhī mūla)	(Rt.)	16 g.
8.	Vacā	(Rz.)	16 g.
9.	Lāṅgalikā	(Pl).	16 g.
10.	Saptaparṇa	(St. Bk.)	16 g.
11.	Suvarcikā (svarjikā kṣāra)		16 g.
12.	Jyotiṣmatī	(Sd.)	16 g.
13.	Taila		768 ml.
14.	Water		3.072 l.

Usage:
Used externally for massage.
Important therapeutic use: Fistula-in-ano and piles.

JĀTYĀDI TAILA
(Śārṅgadharasaṃhitā, Madhyamakhaṇḍa, Adhyāya 9; 168-170.)

1.	Jātī pallava	(Lf.)	192 g.
2.	Nimba pallava	(Lf.)	192 g.
3.	Paṭola pallava	(Lf.)	192 g.
4.	Naktamāla Pallava	(Lf.)	192 g.
5.	Siktha (bee wax)		192 g.
6.	Madhuka (yaṣṭi madhu)	(Rt.)	192 g.
7.	Kuṣṭha	(Rt.)	192 g.

8.	Haridrā	(Rz.)	192 g.
9.	Dāru haridrā	(St.)	192 g.
10.	Kaṭurohiṇī	(Rz.)	192 g.
11.	Mañjiṣṭha	(St.)	192 g.
12.	Padmaka	(Ht. Wd.)	192 g.
13.	Lodhra	(St. Bk.)	192 g.
14.	Abhayā	(Fr. P.)	192 g.
15.	Nīlotpala	(Fl.)	192 g.
16.	Tutthaka		192 g.
17.	Sārivā	(Rt.)	192 g.
18.	Naktamāla bīja	(Sd.)	192 g.
19.	Taila		768 g.
20.	Water		3.072 l.

Usage: Used externally for massage.
Important therapeutic use: Skin diseases.

JYOTIṢMATĪ TAILA

(Yogaratnākara, Kuṣṭhacikitsā; page 696)

1.	Mayūraka (apāmārga) kṣāra jala	(Pt.)	3.072 l.
2.	Jyotiṣmatī taila	(Sd.)	768 g.

Special method of preparation:
Mayūraka kṣāra jala is boiled along with oil till all the moistures evaporates. The process is repeated seven times.

Usage: Used externally for massage.
Important therapeutic use: Leucoderma.

TUṄGADRUMĀDI TAILA

(Sahasrayoga, Tailaprakaraṇa; 43)

1.	Taruṇa tuṅgadruma jala (nārikela)		3.072 l.
2.	Sugandha (śaṭhī)	(Rz.)	96 g.
3.	Lāmajja (uśīra)	(Rt.)	96 g.
4.	Yaṣṭīmadhuka	(Rt.)	96 g.
5.	Utpala (nīlotpala kāṇḍa)		96 g.
6.	Candana (śveta candana)	(Ht. Wd.)	96 g.

7. Dugdha		768 ml.
8. Taila		768 ml.

Usage: Used externally for head-massage.
Important therapeutic use: Head and eye diseases, insomnia.

TUVARAKA TAILA

(Suśrutasaṃhitā, Cikitsāsthāna, Adhyāya 13;.20-23, 29)

1. Tuvaraka phalamajjā taila		768 ml.
2. Khadira kvātha	(Ht. Wd.)	2.304 l.
3. Tuvaraka kalka		128 g.

Special method of preparation:
The prepared *taila* should be kept in *karīṣa* (hot ash of cowdung) for fifteen days before use.
Usage: Used externally for massage.
Pathya: milk, sweets, citrus fruits, apple, banana, sweet grapes, old boiled rice, barely, wheat bread, butter-milk.
Apathya: Sour, saline and pungent substances.
Important therapeutic use: Obstinate skin diseases.

TRIPHALĀDI TAILA

(Sahasrayoga, Tailaprakaraṇa; 44)

1. Harītakī	(Fr. P.)	768 g.
2. Bibhītaka	(Fr. P.)	768 g.
3. Āmalakī	(Fr. P.)	768 g.
4. Amṛtavalli (guḍūcī)	(St.)	768 g.
5. Ketakī mūla	(Rt.)	768 g.
6. Asanaka	(Ht. Wd.)	768 g.
7. Balā	(Rt.)	768 g.
8. Eraṇḍa (mūla)	(Rt.)	768 g.
9. Indra valli (indrāyaṇī)	(Rt.)	768 g.
10. Water for decoction reduced to		12.288 l. 3.072 l.
11. Tekarāja (bhṛṅga rāja) svarasa	(Pt.)	768 ml.
12. Haṭha (āmalakī) svarasa	(Fr. P.)	768 ml.
13. Taila		768 ml.

14. Kṣīra		1.536 l.
15. Kuṣṭha	(Rt.)	128 g.
16. Yaṣṭyāhva	(Rt.)	128 g.
17. Padmaka	(Ht.Wd.)	128 g.
18. Uśīra	(Rt.)	128 g.
19. Candana (śveta candana)	(Ht. Wd.)	128 g.
20. Mustā	(Rz.)	128 g.
21. Elā	(Sd.)	128 g.
22. Patra	(Lf.)	128 g.
23. Māṃsī (jaṭāmāṃsī)	(Rz.)	128 g.
24. Haya gandhā (aśva gandhā)	(Rt.)	128 g.
25. Balā	(Rt.)	128 g.
26. Amṛtā (guḍūcī)	(St.)	128 g.
27. Sārivā	(Rt.)	128 g.
28. Amara kāṣṭha (devadāru)	(Ht. Wd.)	128 g.
29. Lavaṅga	(Fl.)	128 g.
30. Nata (tagara)	(Rt.)	128 g.
31. Coraka (śaṭhī)	(Rz.)	128 g.
32. Śveta kamala	(Fl.)	128 g.
33. Rakta kamala	(Fl.)	128 g.
34. Kumuda	(Fl.)	128 g.
35. Kalhāra	(Fl.)	128 g.
36. Padma	(Fl.)	128 g.
37. Añjana		128 g.
38. Nīlī (mūla)	(Rt.)	128 g.

Usage: Used externally for massage.
Important therapeutic use: Head-diseases, baldness, premature graying of hair, diseases of eye, ear, nose and throat.

DHĀNVANTARA TAILA

(Synonym: Balā taila)

(Vaidyayogaratnāvalī, Tailaprakaraṇa; page 244)

1. Balā mūla	(Rt.)	4.608 g.
2. Water for decoction		36.864 l.
reduced to		4.608 l.
3. Payaḥ (godugdha)		4.608 l.
4. Yava	(Sd.)	768 g.

5. Kola	(Fr.)	768 g.
6. Kulattha	(Sd.)	768 g.
7. Bilva	(Rt.)	768 g.
8. Śyonāka	(Rt.)	768 g.
9. Gambhārī	(Rt.)	768 g.
10. Pāṭalā	(Rt.)	768 g.
11. Gaṇikārikā (agnimantha)	(Rt.)	768 g.
12. Śālaparṇī	(Rt.)	768 g.
13. Pṛśniparṇī	(Rt.)	768 g.
14. Bṛhatī	(Rt.)	768 g.
15. Kaṇṭakārī	(Rt.)	768 g.
16. Gokṣura	(Rt.)	768 g.
17. Water for decoction		6.144 l.
reduced to		768 ml.
18. Taila		768 ml.
19. Medā	(Sub. Rt.)	128 g.
20. Mahā medā	(Rt.)	128 g.
21. Dāru	(Ht. Wd.)	128 g.
22. Mañjiṣṭhā	(St.)	128 g.
23. Kākolī	(Sub. Rt.)	128 g.
24. Kṣīra kākolī	(Sub. Rt.)	128 g.
25. Candana	(Ht. Wd.)	128 g.
26. Śārivā	(Rt.)	128 g.
27. Kuṣṭha	(Rt.)	128 g.
28. Tagara	(Rt.)	128 g.
29. Jīvaka	(Rt.)	128 g.
30. Ṛṣabha	(Sub. Rt.)	128 g.
31. Saindhava		128 g.
32. Kālānusārī	(Sd.)	128 g.
33. Śaileya (śilājatu)		128 g.
34. Vacā	(Rz.)	128 g.
35. Agaru	(Ht. Wd.)	128 g.
36. Punarnavā	(Rt.)	128 g.
37. Aśva gandhā	(Rt.)	128 g.
38. Varī	(Rt.)	128 g.
39. Kṣīra śuklā (kṣīra vidārī)	(Rt. Tr.)	128 g.
40. Yaṣṭī (madhu yaṣṭī)	(Rt.)	128 g.
41. Harītakī	(Fr. P.)	128 g.
42. Āmalakī	(Fr. P.)	128 g.
43. Bibhītaka	(Fr. P.)	128 g.
44. Śatāhavā	(Fl.)	128 g.

45.	Māṣa parṇī	(Pl.)	128 g.
46.	Mudga parṇi	(Pl.)	128 g.
47.	Elā	(Sd.)	128 g.
48.	Tvak	(St. Bk.)	128 g.
49.	Patra	(Lf.)	128 g.

Usage: Used for massage.

Important therapeutic use: Nervous disorders, hemiplegia, paralysis agitans and children diseases.

Note: This taila when prepared with *āvarttana* process is known as *Dhānvantara taila (āvarttita)*.

NĀRĀYAṆA TAILA

(Bhaiṣajyaratnāvalī, Vātavyādhyadhikāra; 140-144 ½)

1.	Bilva	(Rt.)	480 g.
2.	Agnimantha	(Rt.)	480 g.
3.	Śyonāka	(Rt.)	480 g.
4.	Pāṭalā	(Rt.)	480 g.
5.	Pāribhadra	(Rt.)	480 g.
6.	Prasāraṇī	(Pl.)	480 g.
7.	Aśvagandhā	(Rt.)	480 g.
8.	Bṛhatī	(Rt.)	480 g.
9.	Kaṇṭakārī	(Pl.)	480 g.
10.	Balā	(Rt.)	480 g.
11.	Atibalā	(Rt.)	480 g.
12.	Śvadaṃṣṭrā (gokṣura)	(Fr.)	480 g.
13.	Punarnavā	(Rt.)	480 g.
14.	Water for decoction		49.152 l.
	reduced to		12.288 l.
15.	Taila		3.072 l.
16.	Śata puṣpā	(Fl.)	96 g.
17.	Deva dāru	(Ht. Wd.)	96 g.
18.	Māṃsi (jaṭā māṃsī)	(Rz.)	96 g.
19.	Śaileyaka	(Pl.)	96 g.
20	Vacā	(Rz.)	96 g.
21.	Candana	(Ht. Wd.)	96 g.
22.	Tagara	(Rt.)	96 g.
23.	Kuṣṭha	(Rt.)	96 g.
24.	Elā	(Sd.)	96 g.

25. Śāla parṇī	(Rt.)	96 g.
26. Pṛśni parṇī	(Rt.)	96 g.
27. Mudga parṇī	(Rt.)	96 g.
28. Māṣa parṇī	(Rt.)	96 g.
29. Rāsnā	(Rt./Lf.)	96 g.
30. Turaga gandhā (aśvagandhā)	(Rt.)	96 g.
31. Saindhava		96 g.
32. Punarnavā	(Rt.)	96 g.
33. Śatāvarī rasa	(Rt.)	3.072 l.
34. Gavya kṣīra (go kṣīra)		12.288 l.

Usage: Used externally for massage.
Important therapeutic use: Nervous disorders, torticolis and headache.

NĀLPĀMARĀDI TAILA[2]

(Sahasrayoga, Tailaprakaraṇa, 26)

1. Paimaññal (ārdra haridra) rasa	(Rz.)	1.536 l.
2. Parpaṭa rasa	(Pl.)	1.536 l.
3. Eṇṇa (tila taila)		768 ml.
4. Nyagrodha	(St. Bk.)	96 g.
5. Udumbara	(St. Bk.)	96 g.
6. Aśvattha	(St. Bk.)	96 g.
7. Plakṣa	(St. Bk.)	96 g.
8. Harītakī	(Fr. P.)	96 g.
9. Bibhītaka	(Fr. P.)	96 g.
10. Āmalakī	(Fr. P.)	96 g.
11. Candana	(Ht. Wd.)	96 g.
12. Sevya (uśīra)	(Rt.)	96 g.
13. Kuṣṭha	(Rt.)	96 g.
14. Covvalli (mañjiṣṭhā bheda)	(St.)	96 g.
15. Coram (śaṭhī)	(Rz.)	96 g.
16. Akil (agaru)	(Ht. Wd.)	96 g.

Usage: Used externally for massage.
Important therapeutic use: Obstinate skin diseases.

---

2. This formula when prepared with coconut oil is called Nālpāmarādi Kera Taila.

NĪLIKĀDYA TAILA

(Śārṅgadharasaṃhitā, Madhyamakhaṇḍa, Adhyāya 9; 157-160)

1.	Nīlikā	(Pl.)	12 g.
2.	Ketakī kanda	(Rz.)	12 g.
3.	Bhṛṅgarāja	(Pl.)	12 g.
4.	Kuraṇṭaka (sahacara)	(Pl.)	12 g.
5.	Arjuna puṣpa	(Fl.)	12 g.
6.	Bījaka kusuma (asana puṣpa)	(Fl.)	12 g.
7.	Kṛṣṇa tila		12 g.
8.	Tagara	(Rt.)	12 g.
9.	Kamla mūla	(Rt.)	12 g.
10.	Ayoraja (lauha bhasma)		12 g.
11.	Priyaṅgu	(Fl.)	12 g.
12.	Dāḍima tvak	(St. Bk.)	12 g.
13.	Guḍūcikā (guḍūcī)	(St.)	12 g.
14.	Harītakī	(Fr. P.)	12 g.
15.	Bibhītaka	(Fr. P.)	12 g.
16.	Āmalakī	(Fr. P.)	12 g.
17.	Padma paṅka	(Rz.)	12 g.
18.	Taila		768 ml.
19.	Triphalā kvātha	(Fr. P.)	3.072 l.
20.	Bhṛṅgarāja svarasa	(Pl.)	3.072 l.

Usage: Used externally for massage.

Important therapeutic use: Baldness, premature graying of hair, hair fall, skin diseases of the scalp region.

NĪLĪBHṚṄGĀDI TAILA[3]

(Sahasrayoga; Tailaprakaraṇa; 38)

1.	Nīlī (patra) svarasa	(Lf.)	768 ml.
2.	Bhṛṅgarāja svarasa	(Pl.)	768 ml.
3.	Śatakratu latā (indravāruṇī)	(Lf.)	768 ml.
4.	Dhātrī (āmalakī) rasa	(Fr. P.)	768 ml.
5.	Ajā kṣīra		768 ml.

----

3. This yoga when prepared with coconut oil is called Nīlībhṛṅgādi Kera Taila.

6.	Nālikera kṣīra		768 ml.
7.	Mahiṣī kṣīra		768 ml.
8.	Dhenūdbhava (go dugdha)		768 ml.
9.	Taila		768 ml.
10.	Yaṣṭī mathu	(Rt.)	32 g.
11.	Guñjā mūla	(Rt.)	32 g.
12.	Añjana		32 g.

Usage: Used externally for head-massage.
Important therapeutic use: Hair fall, baldness and premature graying of hair.

PARIṆATAKERĪKṢĪRĀDI TAILA
(Sahasrayoga, Tailaprakaraṇa; 9)

1.	Pariṇatakerī (pakva nārikela) kṣīra	(Fr. P)	1.536 l.
2.	Jambīra phalodaka (jambīra rasa)	(Fr.)	1.536 l.
3.	Kṣaṇadā (haridrā)	(Rz.)	48 g.
4.	Suradhūma (sarja rasa)	(Exd.)	48 g.
5.	Taila		768 ml.

Usage: Used externally for massage.
Important therapeutic use: Frozen shoulder and cervical spondylitis.

PIṆḌA TAILA
(Aṣṭāṅgahṛdaya, Cikitsāsthāna, Adhyāya 22; 22)

1.	Madhūcchiṣṭa (bee-wax)		280 g.
2.	Mañjiṣṭhā	(St.)	455 g.
3.	Sarja rasa	(Exd.)	186 g.
4.	Sārivā	(Rt.)	455 g.
5.	Taila		6 l.
6.	Water		24 l.

Special method of preparation:

Sārivā and *mañjiṣṭhā* are taken in the prescribed quantity, powdered and then ground to a fine paste. This is mixed with the prescribed quantity of water. Taila is added and allowed to boil in a vessel sufficiently large to prevent the overflowing when foam is formed. When the required *pāka* is reached, the oil is filtered into a vessel containing the powdered *sarja rasa* and the shavings of *madhūcchiṣṭa* (bees-wax). It is then briskly stirred to enable *sarja rasa* and *madhūcchiṣṭa* to dissolve intimately with the oil so as to form a homogenous liquid.

Usage: Used externally for massage.
Important therapeutic use: Arthritis, gout, and burning sensation.

Note: The quantity of ingredients have been given on the basis of current practice.

PIPPALYĀDI TAILA

(Bhaiṣajyaratnāvalī, Arśorogādhikāra; 115-115½)

1.	Pippalī	(Fr.)	96 g.
2.	Madhuka (Yaṣṭī madhu)	(Rt.)	96 g.
3.	Bilva	(St. Bk.)	96 g.
4.	Śatāhvā	(Fl.)	96 g.
5.	Madana	(Fl.)	96 g.
6.	Vacā	(Rz.)	96 g.
7.	Kuṣṭha	(Rt.)	96 g.
8.	Śaṭhī	(Rz.)	96 g.
9.	Puṣkarākhya (puṣkara mūla)	(Rt.)	96 g.
10.	Citraka	(Rt.)	96 g.
11.	Devadāru	(Ht. Wd.)	96 g.
12.	Taila		768 ml.
13.	Kṣīra		1.536 l.

Usage: Used externally for medicated enema.
Important therapeutic use: Chronic dysentery, prolapse of retum, dysuria and burning micturation.

PRABHAÑJANA VIMARDANA TAILA

(Sahasrayoga, Tailaprakaraṇa; 5)

1.	Balā	(Rt.)	576 g.
2.	Śatāvarī	(Rt.)	576 g.
3.	Śigru	(Rt. Bk.)	576 g.
4.	Varaṇa (varuṇa)	(St. Bk.)	576 g.
5.	Arka (mūla)	(Rt.)	576 g.
6.	Karañjaka (mūla tvak)	(Rt. Bk.	576 g.
7.	Eraṇḍa (mūla)	(Rt.)	576 g.
8.	Koraṇḍa (sahacara)	(Pl.)	576 g.
9.	Vājigandhā (aśvagandhā)	(Rt.)	576 g.
10.	Prasāriṇī	(Pl.)	576 g.
11.	Bilva	(Rt.)	576 g.
12.	Śyonāka	(Rt.)	576 g.
13.	Gambhārī	(Rt.)	576 g.
14.	Pāṭalā	(Rt.)	576 g.
15.	Agnimantha	(Rt.)	576 g.
16.	Water for decoction		24.576 l.
	reduced to		6.144 l.
17.	Taila		1.536 l.
18.	Kṣīra		3.072 l.
19.	Dadhi		1.536 kg.
20.	Kāñjika		1.536 l.
21.	Tagara	(Rt.)	12 g.
22.	Amara kāṣṭha (devadāru)	(Ht. Wd.)	12 g.
23.	Elā	(Sd.)	12 g.
24.	Śuṇṭhī	(Rz.)	12 g.
25.	Sarṣapa	(Sd.)	12 g.
26.	Coraka	(Rz.)	12 g.
27.	Śatāhvā	(Fl.)	12 g.
28.	Kuṣṭha	(Rt.)	12 g.
29.	Sindhūttha (saindhava lavaṇa)		12 g.
30.	Rāsnā	(Rt./Lf.)	12 g.
31.	Kālānusārikā (methī)	(Sd.)	12 g.
32.	Vacā	(Rz.)	12 g.
33.	Citraka	(Rt.)	12 g.
34.	Māṃsī (jaṭā māṃsī)	(Rz.)	12 g.
35.	Sarala	(Rt.)	12 g.
36.	Kaṭurohiṇī	(Rz.)	12 g.

Usage: Used externally for massage.
Important therapeutic use: Paralysis, facial paralysis, multiple sclerosis, spondylitis, arthritis, gout and pain in different parts of the body.

PRASĀRIṆĪ TAILA

(Śārṅgadharasaṃhitā, Madhyamakhaṇḍa, Adhyāya 9; 119-121½)

1. Prasāriṇī	(Pl.)	4.800 kg.
2. Water for decoction		12.288 l.
reduced to		3.072 l.
3. Taila		3.072 l.
4. Dadhi		3.072 kg.
5. Kāñjika		3.072 l.
6. Kṣīra		12.288 l.
7. Madhuka (yaṣṭīmadhu)	(Rt.)	348 g.
8. Pippalīmūla	(Rt.)	348 g.
9. Citraka	(Rt.)	348 g.
10. Saindhava		348 g.
11. Vacā	(Rz.)	348 g.
12. Prasāriṇī	(Pl.)	348 g.
13. Devadāru	(Ht. Wd.)	348 g.
14. Rasnā	(Rt./Lf.)	348 g.
15. Gaja pippalī	(Fr.)	348 g.
16. Bhallāta	(Fr.)	348 g.
17. Śatapuṣpā	(Fr.)	348 g.
18. Māṃsī (jaṭā māṃsī)	(Rz.)	348 g.

Usage: Used externally for massage.
Important therapeutic use: Lumbago, sciatica, torticolis, perkinsonianism, hemiplegia, arthritis, gout and nervous disorders.

BALĀ TAILA

(Aṣṭāṅgahṛdaya, Cikitsāsthāna, Adhyāya 21; 72-78½)

1. Balā	(Rt.)	4.800 kg.
2. Chinnaruhā (guḍūcī)	(St.)	1.200 kg.
3. Rāsnā	(Rt./Lf.)	600 g.

4.	Water for decoction		30.720 l.
	reduced to		3.072 l.
5.	Dadhi mastu		3.072 l.
6.	Ikṣu niryāsa (ikṣu rasa)	(St.)	3.072 l.
7.	Śukta (dhānyāmla)		3.072 l.
8.	Taila		3.072 kg.
9.	Aja payaḥ (ajākṣīra)		1.536 l.
10.	Śaṭhī	(Rz.)	48 g.
11.	Sarala	(Rt.)	48 g.
12.	Dāru (deva dāru)	(Ht. Wd.)	48 g.
13.	Elā	(Sd.)	48 g.
14.	Mañjiṣṭhā	(St.)	48 g.
15.	Agaru	(Ht. Wd.)	48 g.
16.	Candana	(Ht. Wd.)	48 g.
17.	Padmaka	(Ht. Wd.)	48 g.
18.	Atibalā	(Rt.)	48 g.
19.	Mustā	(Rz.)	48 g.
20.	Mudga parṇī	(Pl.)	48 g.
21.	Māṣa parṇī	(Pl.)	48 g.
22.	Hareṇu	(Sd.)	48 g.
23.	Yaṣṭyāhva (yaṣṭīmadhu)	(Rt.)	48 g.
24.	Surasā (tulasī)	(Pl.)	48 g.
25.	Vyāghra nakha		48 g.
26.	Ṛṣabhaka	(Sub. Rt.)	48 g.
27.	Jīvaka	(Rt.)	48 g.
28.	Palāśa rasa (niryāsa)	(Exd.)	48 g.
29.	Kastūrī		48 g.
30.	Nīlikā	(Pl.)	48 g.
31.	Jātīkośa (jāti patrī)	(Adr.)	48 g.
32.	Spṛkkā	(Pl.)	48 g.
33.	Kuṅkuma	(Stl./Stg.)	48 g.
34.	Śaileya	(Pl.)	48 g.
35.	Jātika (jātī phala)	(Sd.)	48 g.
36.	Kaṭphala	(Fr.)	48 g.
37.	Ambu (hrībera)	(Rt.)	48 g.
38.	Tvak	(St. Bk.)	48 g.
39.	Kuṅduruṣka	(Exd.)	48 g.
40.	Karpūra		48 g.
41.	Turuṣka	(Sd.)	48 g.
42.	Śrīnivāsaka (gandhavirajā)		48 g.

43.	Lavaṅga	(Fl.)	48 g.
44.	Nakha		48 g.
45.	Kaṅkola	(Rz.)	48 g.
46.	Kuṣṭha	(Rt.)	48 g.
47.	Māṃsī (jaṭā māṃsī)	(Rz.0	48 g.
48.	Priyaṅgu	(Fl.)	48 g.
49.	Sthauṇeya		48 g.
50.	Tagara	(Rt.)	48 g.
51.	Dhyāma (rohiṣa)	(Pl.)	48 g.
52.	Vacā	(Rz.)	48 g.
53.	Madanaka	(Fr.)	48 g.
54.	Plava (bhadramustaka)	(Rt.)	48 g.
55.	Nāga kesara	(Fl.)	48 g.

Usage: Used externally for massage.
Importand therapeutic use: Chronic fever, paralysis, high blood pressure and burning sensation.

BALĀGUḌŪCYĀDI TAILA

(Sahasrayoga, Tailaprakaraṇa; 14)

1.	Balā	(Rt.)	256 g.
2.	Guḍūcī	(St.)	256 g.
3.	Sura pādapa (deva dāru)	(Ht. Wd.)	256 g.
4.	Water for decoction		12.288 l.
	reduced to		3.072 l.
5.	Jaṭā (jaṭāmāṃsī)	(Rz.)	16 g.
6.	Āmaya (kuṣṭha)	(Rt.)	16 g.
7.	Candana	(Ht. Wd.)	16 g.
8.	Kunduruṣka	(Exd.)	16 g.
9.	Nata (tagara)	(Rt.)	16 g.
10.	Aśvagandhā	(Rt.)	16 g.
11.	Sarala	(Rt.)	16 g.
12.	Rāsnā	(Rt.)	16 g.
13.	Taila		768 ml.

Usage: Used externally for massage.
Important therapeutic use: Gout, rheumatism, osteo-arthritis and skin disorders.

BALĀDHĀTRYĀDI TAILA

(Sahasrayoga, Tailaprakaraṇa; 57)

1.	Balā	(Rt.)	768 g.
2.	Dhātrī (āmalakī)	(Fr.)	768 g.
3.	Guḍūcī	(Sd.)	768 g.
4.	Uśīra	(Rt.)	384 g.
5.	Hiruberaka (hrīvera)	(Rt.)	192 g.
6.	Candana (rakta candana)	(Ht. Wd.)	96 g.
7.	Yaṣṭī (yaṣṭīmadhu)	(Rt.)	96 g.
8.	Bakula prasūna	(Fl.)	96 g.
9.	Water for decoction		12.288 l.
	reduced to		3.072 l.
10.	Madhuka (yaṣṭī madhu)	(Rt.)	96 g.
11.	Rakta candana	(Ht. Wd.)	96 g.
12.	Śveta candana	(Ht. Wd.)	96 g.
13.	Kuṣṭha	(Rt.)	96 g.
14.	Utpala (nīlotpala)	(Fl.)	96 g.
15.	Abda (mustā)	(Rz.)	96 g.
16.	Sārivā	(Rt.)	96 g.
17.	Tvak	(St. Bk.)	96 g.
18.	Elā	(Sd.)	96 g.
19.	Patra	(Lf.)	96 g.
20.	Jātī phala	(Sd.)	96 g.
21.	Takkola	(Rz.)	96 g.
22.	Karpūra	(Exd.)	96 g.
23.	Śatāvarī	(Rt.)	96 g.
24.	Jīvaka	(Rt.)	96 g.
25.	Ṛṣabhaka	(Sub. Rt.)	96 g.
26.	Medā	(Sub. Rt.)	96 g.
27.	Mṛdvīkā	(Dr. Fr.)	96 g.
28.	Kuṅkuma	(Stl./Stg.)	96 g.
29.	Lāmajjaka	(Rt.)	96 g.
30.	Śālūka (kamala kanda)	(Rz.)	96 g.
31.	Śaṭhī	(Rz.)	96 g.
32.	Caṇḍā kanda (kacūraka)	(Rz.)	96 g.
33.	Puṣkara (puṣkara mūla)	(Rt.)	96 g.
34.	Nāga puṣpa	(Fl.)	96 g.
35.	Nakha		96 g.
36.	Spṛkkā	(Pl.)	96 g.

37. Mañjiṣṭhā	(St.)	96 g.
38. Kaṭurohiṇī (kaṭukā)	(Rz.)	96 g.
39. Añjana		96 g.
40. Sarala	(St.)	96 g.
41. Dāru (devadāru)	(Ht. Wd.)	96 g.
42. Campaka puṣpa	(Fl).	96 g.
43. Mṛga nābhi (gandha mārjāravīrya)		96 g.
44. Madhūka puṣpa	(Fl.)	96 g.
45. Śyonāka	(Pl.)	96 g.
46. Harītakī	(Fr. P.)	96 g.
47. Bibhītaka	(Fr. P.)	96 g.
48. Āmalakī	(Fr. P.)	96 g.
49. Phalinī puṣpa	(Fl.)	96 g.
50. Misi	(Fr.)	96 g.
51. Mustā	(Rz.)	96 g.
52. Agaru	(Ht. Wd.)	96 g.
53. Māṃsī (jaṭā māṃsī)	(Rt.)	96 g.
54. Tagara	(Rz.)	96 g.
55. Padma kesara	(Adr.)	96 g.
56. Kṣīra		768 ml.
57. Āmalakī rasa	(Fr.)	768 ml.
58. Śatāvarī rasa	(Rt.)	768 ml.
59. Taila		768 ml.

Usage: Used externally for massage.

Important therapeutic use: Tuberculosis, eye diseases, nervous disorders.

BALĀŚVAGANDHALĀKṢĀDI TAILA

(Sahasrayoga, Tailaprakaraṇa; 13)

1. Balā	(Rt.)	768 g.
2. Aśvagandhā	(Rt.)	768 g.
3. Lākṣā	(Exd.)	768 g.
4. Water for decoction		12.288 l.
reduced to		3.072 l.
5. Taila		768 ml.
6. Dadhi mastu		3.072 l.
7. Rāsnā	(Rt./Lf.)	12 g.

8.	Candana	(Ht. Wd.)	12 g.
9.	Mañjiṣṭhā	(St.)	12 g.
10.	Dūrvā	(Rt.)	12 g.
11.	Madhuka (yaṣṭīmadhu)	(Rt.)	12 g.
12.	Coraka	(Pl.)	12 g.
13.	Sārivā	(Rt.)	12 g.
14.	Uśīra	(Rt.)	12 g.
15.	Jalada (mustā)	(Rz.)	12 g.
16.	Kuṣṭha	(Rt.)	12 g.
17.	Agaru	(Ht. Wd.)	12 g.
18.	Sura druma (deva dāru)	(Ht. Wd.)	12 g.
19.	Haridrā	(Rz.)	12 g.
20.	Kumudā (kanda)	(Rz.)	12 g.
21.	Kauntī (reṇukā bīja)	(Sd.)	12 g.
22.	Śatāhvā	(Fl.)	12 g.
23.	Padma kesara	(Adr.)	12 g.

Special Method of preparation:

Lākṣa is powdered well and placed in a vessel. Hot water is poured and stirred well. When the water becomes red it is strained and used.

Usage: Used externally for massage.

Important therapeutic use: Fever, pseudomuscular distrophy, epilepsy and psyzophrenia.

BALĀHAṬHĀDI TAILA

(Sahasrayoga, Tailaprakaraṇa; 54)

1.	Balā	(Rt.)	768 g.
2.	Haṭha (āmalakī)	(Fr. P.)	768 g.
3.	Amṛtā (guḍūcī)	(St.)	768 g.
4.	Mudga	(Sd.)	768 g.
5.	Māṣa	(Sd.)	768 g.
6.	Water for decoction		12.288 l.
	reduced to		3.072 l.
7.	Tilodbhava (tila taila)		768 ml.
8.	Candana (śveta candana)	(Ht. Wd.)	128 g.
9.	Āmaya (kuṣṭha)	(Rt.)	128 g.
10.	Yaṣṭī (yaṣṭīmadhu)	(Rt.)	128 g.

Special Method of preparation:
Mudga and *māṣa* are boiled together till they become very soft. The decoction is strained and used.
Usage: Used externally for head-massage.
Important therapeutic use: Headache and refraction errors of eyes.

BṚHAT GUḌŪCĪ TAILA

(Bhaiṣajyaratnāvalī, Vātaraktādhikāra; 53-56½)

1.	Chinnaruhā (guḍūcī)	(St.)	4.800 kg.
2.	Water for decoction		12.288 l.
	reduced to		3.072 l.
3.	Taila		768 ml.
4.	Kṣīra		3.072 l.
5.	Aśvagandhā	(Rt.)	12 g.
6.	Vidārī	(Rt. Tr.)	12 g.
7.	Kākolī	(Sub. Rt.)	12 g.
8.	Kṣīra kākolī	(Sub. Rt.)	12 g.
9.	Hari candana	(Ht. Wd.)	12 g.
10.	Śatāvarī	(Rt.)	12 g.
11.	Atibalā	(Rt.)	12 g.
12.	Śvadaṃṣṭrā (gokṣura)	(Fr.)	12 g.
13.	Bṛhatī	(Rt.)	12 g.
14.	Kaṇṭakārī	(Pl.)	12 g.
15.	Kṛmighna (viḍaṅga)	(Fr.)	12 g.
16.	Harītakī	(Fr. P.)	12 g.
17.	Bibhītaka	(Fr. P.)	12 g.
18.	Āmalakī	(Fr. P.)	12 g.
19.	Rāsnā	(Rt./Lf.)	12 g.
20.	Trāyamāṇā	(Pl.)	12 g.
21.	Śārivā	(Rt.)	12 g.
22.	Jīvantī	(Rt.)	12 g.
23.	Granthika (pippalīmūla)	(Rt.)	12 g.
24.	Śuṇṭhī	(Rz.)	12 g.
25.	Marica	(Fr.)	12 g.
26.	Pippalī	(Fr.)	12 g.
27.	Bākucī (bīja)	(Sd.)	12 g.
28.	Bhekaparṇikā		

	(maṇḍūka parṇī)	(Pl.)	12 g
29.	Viśālā (indrāyaṇa mūla)	(Pl.)	12 g
30.	Granthiparṇa	(Rt.)	12 g
31.	Mañjiṣṭhā	(St.)	12 g
32.	Candana (rakta candana)	(Ht. Wd.)	12 g
33.	Niśā (haridrā)	(Rz.)	12 g
34.	Śatāhvā (śatapuṣpā)	(Pl.)	12 g
35.	Sapta parṇī	(St. Bk.)	12 g

Usage: Used externally for massage.

Important therapeutic use: Gout, arthritis and obstinate skin diseases.

BṚHAT MĀṢA TAILA

(Bhaiṣajyaratnāvalī, Vātavyādhyadhikāra; 241-242½)

1.	Taila		768 ml.
2.	Māṣa	(Sd.)	768 g.
3.	Water for decoction		3.072 l.
	reduced to		768 ml.
4.	Balā	(Rt.)	768 g.
5.	Water for decoction		3.072 l.
	reduced to		768 ml.
6.	Rāsnā	(Rt./Lf.)	768 g.
7.	Water for decoction		3.072 l.
	reduced to		768 ml.
8.	Daśamūla	(Rt.)	768 g.
9.	Water for decoction		3.072 l.
	reduced to		768 ml.
10.	Yava	(Sd.)	256 g.
11.	Kola (badara)	(Sd.)	256 g.
12.	Kulattha	(Sd.)	256 g.
13.	Water for decoction		3.072 l.
	reduced to		768 ml.
14.	Chāga māṃsa (Goat's meat)		768 g.
15.	Water for decoction		3.072 l.
	reduced to		768 ml.
16.	Kṣīra		3.072 l.
17.	Rāsnā	(Rt./Lf.)	12 g.
18.	Ātmaguptā	(Sd.)	12 g.

19.	Sindhūttha (saindhava lavaṇa)		12 g.
20.	Śatāhva	(Fl.)	12 g.
21.	Eraṇḍa	(Rt.)	12 g.
22.	Mustaka	(Rz.)	12 g.
23.	Jīvaka	(Rt.)	12 g.
24.	Ṛṣabhaka	(Sub. Rt.)	12 g.
25.	Medā	(Sub. Rt.)	12 g.
26.	Mahā medā	(Rt.)	12 g.
27.	Kākolī	(Sub. Rt.)	12 g.
28.	Kṣira kākolī	(Sub. Rt.)	12 g.
29.	Ṛddhī	(Sub. Rt. Tr.)	12 g.
30.	Vṛddhi	(Sub. Rt. Tr.)	12 g.
31.	Madhu yaṣṭī	(Rt.)	12 g.
32.	Jivantī	(Rt.)	12 g.
33.	Mudga parṇī	(Pl.)	12 g.
34.	Māṣa parṇī	(Pl.)	12 g.
35.	Balā	(Rt.)	12 g.
36.	Śuṇṭhī	(Rz.)	12 g.
37.	Marica	(Fr.)	12 g.
38.	Pippalī	(Fr.)	12 g.

Usage: Used externally for massage.

Important therapeutic use: Facial paralysis, paralysis agitans, multiple sclerosis, sciatica and osteo-arthritis.

BṚHAT SAINDHAVĀDYA TAILA

(Bhaiṣajyaratnāvalī, Āmavātādhikāra; 157-159)

1.	Saindhava		24 g.
2.	Śreyasī (gaja pippalī)	(Fr.)	24 g.
3.	Rāsnā	(Rt./Lf.)	24 g.
4.	Śata puṣpā	(Fl.)	24 g.
5.	Yamānikā	(Fr.)	24 g.
6.	Sarjikā	(Exd.)	24 g.
7.	Marica	(Fr.)	24 g.
8.	Kuṣṭha	(Rt.)	24 g.
9.	Śuṇṭhī	(Rz.)	24 g.
10.	Sauvarcala		24 g.
11.	Viḍa		24 g.

12.	Vacā	(Rz.)	24 g.
13.	Ajamodā	(Fr.)	24 g.
14.	Madhuka (yaṣṭīmadhu)	(Rt.)	24 g.
15.	Jīraka	(Fr.)	24 g.
16.	Pauṣkara (puṣkarȧ mūla)	(Rt.)	24 g.
17.	Kaṇā (pippalī)	(Fr.)	24 g.
18.	Eraṇḍa taila		768 ml.
19.	Śatapuṣpajāmbu (śata puṣpa kaṣāya)	(Fl.)	768 ml.
20.	Kāñjika		1.536 l.
21.	Mastu		1.536 l.

Usage: Used externally for massage.
Important therapeutic use: Hemiplegia, facial paralysis, sciatica, rheumatic arthritis, osteo-arthritis and heart diseases.

BHṚṄGĀMALAKĀDI TAILA
(Sahasrayoga, Tailaprakaraṇa; 56)

1.	Bhṛṅga rasa (bhṛṅgarāja svarasa)	(Pl.)	768 ml.
2.	Āmalaka rasa	(Fr. P.)	768 ml.
3.	Taila		768 ml.
4.	Kṣīra		3.072 l.
5.	Madhuka (yaṣṭīmadhu)	(Rt.)	48 g.

Usage: Used externally for head-massage.
Important therapeutic use: Aphasia, deafness, cataract, baldness, premature graying of hair, tooth-diseases and insomnia.

Note: If prepared with coconut oil the name will be *Bhṛgāmalakādi Kera Taila*.

BHṚṄGARĀJA TAILA
(Bhaiṣajyaratnāvalī, Kṣudrarogādhikāra; 91-93½)

1.	Taila		768 ml.
2.	Mārkava (bhṛṅga rāja svarasa)	(Pl.)	3.072 l.

3.	Mañjiṣṭhā	(St.)	48 g.
4.	Padmaka	(Ht. Wd.)	48 g.
5.	Lodhra	(St. Bk.)	48 g.
6.	Candana	(Ht. Wd.)	48 g.
7.	Gairika		48 g.
8.	Balā	(Rt.)	48 g.
9.	Haridā	(Rz.)	48 g.
10.	Dāru haridrā	(St.)	48 g.
11.	Keśara (nāga keśara)	(Fl.)	48 g.
12.	Priyaṅgu	(Fl.)	48 g.
13.	Madhu yaṣṭī	(Rt.)	48 g.
14.	Prapauṇḍarīka	(Rt.)	48 g.
15.	Gopī (śārivā)	(Rt.)	48 g.

Usage: Used externally for head-massage.
Important therapeutic use: Diseases of head, eyes, ears and hair.

MAÑJIṢṬHĀDI TAILA

(Sahasrayoga, Tailaprakaraṇa; 50)

1.	Mañjiṣṭhā	(St.)	96 g.
2.	Añjana	(St. Bk.)	96 g.
3.	Śārivā	(Rt.)	96 g.
4.	Abda (mustā)	(Rz.)	96 g.
5.	Kaṭuka (kaṭu rohiṇī)	(Rz.)	96 g.
6.	Takkola (mūla)	(Rt.)	96 g.
7.	Jātī phala	(Sd.)	96 g.
8.	Śrīkaṇṭha (rakta candana)	(Ht. Wd.)	96 g.
9.	Harītakī	(Fr. P.)	96 g.
10.	Bibhītaka	(Fr. P.)	96 g.
11.	Āmalakī	(Fr. P.)	96 g.
12.	Jaṭā (jaṭā māṃsī)	(Rz.)	96 g.
13.	Tagara	(Rt.)	96 g.
14.	Ruk (kuṣṭha)	(Rz.)	96 g.
15.	Yaṣṭī	(Rt.)	96 g.
16.	Tvak	(St. Bk.)	96 g.
17.	Elā	(Sd.)	96 g.
18.	Patra	(Lf.)	96 g.
19.	Nāga keśara	(Fl.)	96 g.

20.	Uśīra	(Rt.)	96 g.
21.	Aragu	(Ht. Wd.)	96 g.
22.	Śaṭhī	(Rz.)	96 g.
23.	Caṇḍā	(Rz.)	96 g.
24.	Mṛga nābhi (gandha-mārjāra-vīrya)		96 g.
25.	Indu (karpūra)	(Exd.)	96 g.
26.	Utpala	(Fl.)	96 g.
27.	Ambhas (hrībera)	Rt.)	96 g.
28.	Bisa (kamala nāla) (Com. Tiss.)		96 g.
29.	Taila		768 ml.
30.	Payaḥ		768 ml.
31.	Kumārī rasa		768 ml.

Usage: Used externally for massage.
Important therapeutic use: Headache, giddiness and pain in eyes.

MADHUYAṢṬYĀDI TAILA

(Aṣṭāṅgahṛdaya, Cikitsāsthāna, Adhyāya 22; 41-43½)

1.	Maddhu yaṣṭī	(Rt.)	4.800 kg.
2.	Water for decoction		19.200 l.
	reduced to		4.800 l.
3.	Taila		3.072 l.
4.	Kṣīra		3.072 l.
5.	Sthirā (śāla parṇī)	(Pl.)	24 kg.
6.	Tāmalakī (bhūmyāmalakī)	(Pl.)	24 g.
7.	Dūrvā	(Rt.)	24 g.
8.	Payasa (kṣīra vidārī)	(Rt. Tr.)	24 g.
9.	Abhīru (śatāvarī)	(Rt.)	24 g.
10.	Candana	(Ht. Wd.)	24 g.
11.	Loha (agaru)	(Ht. Wd.)	24 g.
12.	Haṃsapadī	(Pl.)	24 g.
13.	Māṃsī (jaṭā māṃsī)	(Rz.)	24 g.
14.	Medā	(Sub. Rt.)	24 g.
15.	Mahāmedā	(Rt.)	24 g.
16.	Madhu parṇī (guḍūcī)	(St.)	24 g.
17.	Kākolī	(Sub. Rt.)	24 g.

18.	Kṣīra kākolī	(Sub. Rt.)	24 g.
19.	Śatapuṣpā	(Pl.)	24 g.
20.	Ṛddhi	(Pl.)	24 g.
21.	Padmaka	(Sub. Rt. Tr.)	24 g.
22.	Jīvaka	(Rt.)	24 g.
23.	Ṛṣabha	(Sub. Rt.)	24 g.
24.	Jīvantī	(Rt.)	24 g.
25.	Tvak	(St. Bk.)	24 g.
26.	Patra (teja patra)	(Lf.)	24 g.
27.	Nakha		24 g.
28.	Bālaka (hrībera)	(Rt.)	24 g.
29.	Prapauṇḍarīka	(Rt.)	24 g.
30.	Mañjiṣṭhā	(St.)	24 g.
31.	Sārivā	(Rt.)	24 g.
32.	Aindrī (indra vāruṇī)	(Rt.)	24 g.
33.	Vitunnaka (dhānyaka)	(Fr.)	24 g.

Usage: Used externally for massage and medicated enema.

Important therapeutic use: Burning sensation, gout and arthritis.

MAHĀ NĀRĀYAṆA TAILA

(Bhaiṣajyaratnāvalī, Vātavyādhyadhikāra; 151-157)

1.	Bilva	(Rt.)	960 g.
2.	Aśvagandhā	(Rt.)	960 g.
3.	Bṛhatī mūla	(Rt.)	960 g.
4.	Śvadaṃṣṭrā (gokṣura)	(Rt.)	960 g.
5.	Śyonāka	(Rt.)	960 g.
6.	Vāṭyālaka (balā)	(Rt.)	960 g.
7.	Pāribhadra	(Rt.)	960 g.
8.	Kṣudrā (kaṇṭakārī)	(Pl.)	960 g.
9.	Kaṭhilla (punarnavā)	(Rt.)	960 g.
10.	Atibalā	(Rt.)	960 g.
11.	Agnimantha	(Rt.)	960 g.
12.	Saraṇī (prasāraṇī)	(Pl.)	960 g.
13.	Pāṭalī	(Rt.)	960 g.
14.	Water for decoction		98.304 l.
	reduced to		24.576 l.

15. Taila		6.144 l.
16. Ajā dugdha or Go dugdha		6.144 l.
17. Śatāvarī rasa	(Rt.)	6.144 l.
18. Rāsnā	(Rt./Lf.)	96 g.
19. Aśvagandhā	(Rt.)	96 g.
20. Misī	(Fr.)	96 g.
21. Dāru (devadāru)	(Ht. Wd.)	96 g.
22. Kuṣṭha	(Rt.)	96 g.
23. Śāla parṇī	(Pl.)	96 g.
24. Pṛśni parṇī	(Pl.)	96 g.
25. Mudga parṇī	(Pl.)	96 g.
26. Māṣa parṇī	(Pl.)	96 g.
27. Agaru	(Ht. Wd.)	96 g.
28. Keśara (nāga keśara)	(Fl.)	96 g.
29. Sindhūttha (saindhava)		96 g.
30. Māṃsī (jaṭā māṃsī)	(Rz.)	96 g.
31. Haridrā	(Rz.)	96 g.
32. Dāru haridrā	(St.)	96 g.
33. Śaileyaka	(Rt.)	96 g.
34. Candana	(Ht. Wd.)	96 g.
35. Puṣkara (puṣkara mūla)	(Rt.)	96 g.
36. Elā	(Sd.)	96 g.
37. Asra (mañjiṣṭhā)	(St.)	96 g.
38. Yaṣṭī (yaṣṭīmadhu)	(Rt.)	96 g.
39. Tagara	(Rt.)	96 g.
40. Abda (mustā)	(Rz.)	96 g.
41. Patra (teja patra)	(Lf.)	96 g.
42. Bhṛṅga (bhṛṅga rāja)	(Pl.)	96 g.
43. Jīvaka	(Rt.)	96 g.
44. Ṛṣabhaka	(Sub. Rt.)	96 g.
45. Medā	(Sub. Rt.)	96 g.
46. Mahāmedā	(Rt.)	96 g.
47. Kākolī	(Sub. Rt.)	96 g.
48. Kṣīra kākolī	(Sub. Rt.)	96 g.
49. Ṛddhi	(Sub. Rt. Tr.)	96 g.
50. Vṛddhi	(Sub. Rt. Tr.)	96 g.
51. Ambu (hrībera)	(Rt.)	96 g.
52. Vacā	(Rz.)	96 g.
53. Palāśa	(St. Bk.)	96 g.
54. Sthauṇeya	(St. Bk.)	96 g.

55.	Vṛscīraka (śveta punarnavā)	(Rt.)	96 g.
56.	Coraka	(Pl.)	96 g.
57.	Karpūra	(Exd.)	48 g.
58.	Kāśmīra (kesara)	(Adr.)	48 g.
59.	Mṛgāṇḍaja (kastūrī)		48 g.

Usage: Used externally for massage and medicated enema.
Important therapeutic use: Facial paralysis, deafness, torticolis, cervical spondylosis, wasting of muscles, lumbago, arthritis and gout.

MAHĀ VIṢAGARBHA TAILA

(Bhaiṣajyaratnāvalī, Vātavyādhyadhikāra; 414-421)

1.	Taila		768 ml.
2.	Kanaka (dhustūra)	(Rt.)	48 g.
3.	Nirguṇḍī	(Rt.)	48 g.
4.	Tumbinī	(Fr.)	48 g.
5.	Punarnavā	(Rt.)	48 g.
6.	Vātāri (eraṇḍa mūla)	(Rt.)	48 g.
7.	Aśva gandhā	(Rt.)	48 g.
8.	Prapunnāḍa	(Sd.)	48 g.
9.	Citraka	(Rt.)	48 g.
10.	Śobhāñjana (tvak)	(St. Bk.)	48 g.
11.	Kākamācī	(Pl.)	48 g.
12.	Kalikārī (lāṅgalī)	(Rt.)	48 g.
13.	Nimba	(St. Bk.)	48 g.
14.	Mahā nimba	(St. Bk.)	48 g.
15.	Īśvarī	(Rt.)	48 g.
16.	Bilva	(Rt.)	48 g.
17.	Śyonāka	(Rt.)	48 g.
18.	Gambhārī	(Rt.)	48 g.
19.	Pāṭalā	(Rt.)	48 g.
20.	Agnimantha	(Rt.)	48 g.
21.	Śālaparṇī	(Rt.)	48 g.
22.	Pṛśni parṇī	(Rt.)	48 g.
23.	Bṛhatī	(Rt.)	48 g.
24.	Kaṇṭakārī	(Rt.)	48 g.
25.	Gokṣura	(Rt.)	48 g.
26.	Śatāvarī	(Rt.)	48 g.

27. Kāravallī	(Rt.)	48 g.
28. Sārivā	(Rt.)	48 g.
29. Srāvaṇi (muṇḍī)	(St. Bk.)	48 g.
30. Vidārī	(Rt. Tr.)	48 g.
31. Vajra (snuhī mūla)	(Rt.)	48 g.
32. Arka	(Rt.)	48 g.
33. Meṣa śṛṅgī	(Rt.)	48 g.
34. Śveta karavīra	(Rt.)	48 g.
35. Rakta karavīra	(Rt.)	48 g.
36. Vacā	(Rz.)	48 g.
37. Kākajaṅghā	(Sd.)	48 g.
38. Apāmārga	(Rt.)	48 g.
39. Balā	(Rt.)	48 g.
40. Ati balā	(Rt.)	48 g.
41. Nāga balā	(Rt.)	48 g.
42. Vyāghrī	(Rt.)	48 g.
43. Mahā balā	(Rt.)	48 g.
44. Vāsā	(Rt.)	48 g.
45. Somavallī	(Rt.)	48 g.
46. Prasāraṇī	(Pl.)	48 g.
47. Water for decoction		12.288 l.
reduced to		3.288 l.
48. Śuṇṭhī	(Rz.)	192 g.
49. Marica	(Fr.)	192 g.
50. Pippalī	(Fr.)	192 g.
51. Viṣa tindu (kupīlu)	(Rt.)	192 g.
52. Rāsnā	(Rt./Lf.)	192 g.
53. Kuṣṭha	(Rt.)	192 g.
54. Viṣa (śṛṅgī viṣa)	(Gl.)	192 g.
55. Ghana (mustaka)	(Rz.)	192 g.
56. Devadāru	(Ht. Wd.)	192 g.
57. Vatsanābha	(Rt.)	192 g.
58. Yava kṣāra		192 g.
59. Svarjikā kṣāra		192 g.
60. Saindhava		192 g.
61. Sauvarcala		192 g.
62. Viḍa		192 g.
63. Audbhida		192 g.
64. Sāmudra		192 g.
65. Tutthaka		192 g.
66. Kaṭphala	(Fr.)	192 g.

67.	Pāṭhā	(Rt.)	192 g.
68.	Bhārṅgī	(Rt.)	192 g.
69.	Navasādara	(Rt.)	192 g.
70.	Trāyantī	(Pl.)	192 g.
71.	Dhanvayāsa	(Pl.)	192 g.
72.	Jīraka	(Fr.)	192 g.
73.	Indravāruṇī	(Rt.)	192 g.

Usage: Used externally for massage.

Important therapeutic use: Nervous disorders, hemiplegia, facial paralysis, sciatica, arthritis and general neuralgia.

YAṢṬĪMADHUKA TAILA

(Śārṅgadharasaṃhitā, Madhyamakhaṇḍa, Adhyāya 9; 155-155½)

1.	Taila		768 ml.
2.	Yaṣṭī madhuka	(Rt.)	96 g.
3.	Kṣīra		3.072 l.
4.	Dhātrī phala (svarasa)	(Fr.)	3.072 l.

Usage: Used externally for massage.

Important therapeutic use: Baldness and premature graying of hair.

LAGHU VIṢAGARBHA TAILA

(Bhaiṣajyaratnāvalī, Vātavyādhyadhikāra; 411-412.)

1.	Taila		3.072 l.
2.	Dhattūra svarasa	(Lf.)	960 ml.
3.	Kāñjika		3.072 l.
4.	Gada (kuṣṭha)	(Rt.)	90 g.
5.	Vacā	(Rz.)	90 g.
6.	Hṛddhātrī (bhūmyāmalakī)	(Pl.)	27 g.
7.	Marica	(Fr.)	27 g.
8.	Viṣa (vatsanābha)	(Rz.)	18 g.
9.	Svarṇa (dhattūra) bīja	(Sd.)	81 g.
10.	Paṭu (saindhava)		81 g.

Usage: Used externally for massage.

Important therapeutic use: Nervous disorders, lumbago, torticolis, hemiplegia, paraplegia and lock-jaw.

LĀKṢĀDI TAILA

(Bhaiṣajyaratnāvalī, Jvarādhikāra; 346)

1. Tail		768 ml.
2. Āranāla		4.608 l.
3. Lākṣā	(Exd.)	32 g.
4. Haridrā	(Rz.)	32 g.
5. Mañjiṣṭhā	(St.)	32 g.

Usage: Used externally for massage.
Important therapeutic use: Chronic fever and burning sensation.

LĀṄGALĪ TAILA

(Synonym : Nirguṇḍī Taila)
(Śārṅgadharasaṃhitā, Madhyamakhaṇḍa, Adhyāya 9; 198)

1. Nirguṇḍīsvarasa	(Lf.)	3.072 l.
2. Taila		768 ml.
3. Lāṅgalī mūla	(Rt.)	96 g.

Usage: Used externally for massage.
Important therapeutic use: Tubercular lymphadenitis.

VACĀDI TAILA

(Aṣṭāṅgahṛdaya, Uttarasthāna, Adhyāya 30; 25)

1. Vacā	(Rz.)	192 g.
2. Harītakī	(Fr. P.)	192 g.
3. Lākṣā	(Exd.)	192 g.
4. Kaṭurohiṇī	(Rz.)	192 g.
5. Candana	(Ht. Wd.)	192 g.
6. Taila		768 ml.
7. Water		4.072 l.

Usage: Applied externally.
Important therapeutic use: Tubercular lymphadenitis.

VACĀLAŚUNĀDI TAILA

(Sahasrayoga, Tailaprakaraṇa; 42)

1.	Vacā	(Rz.)	32 g.
2.	Laśuna	(Bl.)	32 g.
3.	Doṣā (haridrā)	(Rz.)	32 g.
4.	Bilva patra rasa	(Lf.)	3.072 l.
5.	Taila		768 ml.

Usage: Used externally as ear-drops and head-massage.
Important therapeutic use: Otitis media, earache and deafness.

VAJRAKA TAILA

(Aṣṭāṅgahṛdaya, Cikitsāsthāna, Adhyāya 9, 79-80)

1.	Śaptāhavā (saptaparṇa mūla tvak)	(Rt. Bk.)	192 g.
2.	Śirīṣa	(Sd.)	192 g.
3.	Aśvamāra (karavīra)	(Rt.)	192 g.
4.	Arka	(Rt.)	192 g.
5.	Mālatī	(Fl.)	192 g.
6.	Citraka	(Rt.)	192 g.
7.	Āsphoṭaka (sārivā)	(Rt.)	192 g.
8.	Nimba	(St. Bk.)	192 g.
9.	Karañja bīja	(Sd.)	192 g.
10.	Sarṣapa	(Sd.)	192 g.
11.	Prapunnāṭa	(Sd.)	192 g.
12.	Harītakī	(Fr. P.)	192 g.
13.	Bibhītaka	(Fr. P.)	192 g.
14.	Āmalakī	(Fr. P.)	192 g.
15.	Jantughna (viḍaṅga)	(Fr.)	192 g.
16.	Śuṇṭhī	(Rz.)	192 g.
17.	Marica	(Fr.)	192 g.
18.	Pippalī	(Fr.)	192 g.
19.	Haridrā	(Rz.)	192 g.
20.	Dāru haridrā	(St.)	192 g.
21.	Taila		768 ml.
22.	Mūtra (cow's urine)		3.072 l.

Usage: Used externally for massage.
Important therapeuticc use: Obstinate skin diseases.

VĀSĀCANDANĀDI TAILA

(Bhaiṣajyaratnāvalī, Kāsādhikāra; 185-189)

1.	Candana	(Ht. Wd.)	48 g.
2.	Reṇukā	(Sd.)	48 g.
3.	Pūti (karañja bīja)	(Sd.)	48 g.
4.	Haya gandhā (aśva gandhā)	(Rt.)	48 g.
5.	Prasāraṇī	(Pl.)	48 g.
6.	Tvak	(St. Bk.)	48 g.
7.	Elā	(Sd.)	48 g.
8.	Patra	(Lf.)	48 g.
9.	Kaṇā mūla (pippalī mūla)	(Rt.)	48 g.
10.	Nāga kesara	(Fl.)	48 g.
11.	Medā	(Sub. Rt.)	48 g.
12.	Mahā medā	(Rt.)	48 g.
13.	Śuṇṭhī	(Rz.)	48 g.
14.	Marica	(Fr.)	48 g.
15.	Pippalī	(Fr.)	48 g.
16.	Rāsnā	(Rt./Lf.)	48 g.
17.	Madhuka	(Fl.)	48 g.
18.	Śailaja (śilājatu)		48 g.
19.	Śaṭhī	(Rz.)	48 g.
20.	Kuṣṭha	(Rz.)	48 g.
21.	Devadāru	(Ht.Wd.)	48 g.
22.	Vanitā (priyaṅgu)	(Fl.)	48 g.
23.	Bibhītaka	(Fr. P.)	48 g.
24.	Taila		3.072 l.
25.	Vāsā	(Rt.)	4.800 kg.
26.	Water for decoction		12.288 l.
	reduced to		3.072 l.
27.	Lākṣā rasa	(Exd.)	3.072 l.
28.	Dadhi mastu		3.072 l.
29.	Candana	(Ht. Wd.)	192 g.
30.	Amṛtā (guḍūcī)	(St.)	192 g.
31.	Bhārṅgī	(Rt.)	192 g.
32.	Daśa mūla	(Rt.)	192 g.
33.	Water for decoction		12.288 l.
	reduced to		3.072 l.

Usage: Used externally for massage.

Important therapeutic use: Bronchitis, asthma, chronic fever, anemia, jaundice, tuberculosis and bleeding from different parts of the body.

VIṢATINDUKA TAILA

(Bhaiṣajyaratnāvalī, Vātaraktādhikāra; 76-77)

1.	Viṣa taru (viṣatinduka) (phalamajjā kaṣāya)	(Fr. p.)	1.535 l.
2.	Śigru svarasa	(Lf.)	768 ml.
3.	Lakuca vāri (kaṣāya)	(Rt.)	768 ml.
4.	Kanaka (dhattūra) svarasa	(Lf.)	1.535 l.
5.	Varuṇa patra svarasa	(Lf.)	1.535 l.
6.	Citrā (citraka) patra svarasa	(Lf.)	1.535 l.
7.	Nirguṇḍikā svarasa	(Lf.)	1.535 l.
8.	Snuk (snuhī svarasa)	(St.)	1.535 l.
9.	Turaga gandhā (aśva gandhā) kaṣāya	(Rt.)	1.535 l.
10.	Vaijayantī rasa	(Lf.)	1.535 l.
11.	Taila		1.535 l.
12.	Laśuna	(Bl.)	192 g.
13.	Sarala	(St.)	192 g.
14.	Yaṣṭī (madhu yaṣṭī)	(Rt.)	192 g.
15.	Kuṣṭha	(Rt.)	192 g.
16.	Saindhava		192 g.
17.	Viḍa		192 g.
18.	Dahana (citraka)	(Rt.)	192 g.
19.	Timira (haridrā)	(Rz.)	192 g.
20.	Kṛṣṇā (pippali)	(Fr.)	192 g.

Usage: Used externally for massage.

Important therapeutic use: Nervous disorders, rheumatic and rheumatoid arthritis, osteo-arthritis and gout.

VRAṆARĀKṢASA TAILA

((Bhaiṣajyaratnāvalī, Vātaraktādhikāra; 69-69½)

1.	Sūtaka (pārada)	12 g.
2.	Gandhaka	12 g.

3.	Tāla (haratāla)		12 g.
4.	Sindūra		12 g.
5.	Manaḥśilā		12 g.
6.	Rasona	(Bl.)	12 g.
7.	Viṣa (vatsanābha)	(Rz.)	12 g.
8.	Tāmra (cūrṇa)		12 g.
9.	Sarṣapa taila		192 ml.

Special method of preparation:
Kajjalī is prepared first and the rest of the drugs are powdered and mixed well with the *kajjalī*. This powder is added to the *sarṣapa taila* and kept under the sun rays for severn days.

Usage: Used externally for massage.

Important therapeutic use: Burning sensations, eczema, psoriasis, sinus, tubercular adenitis and obstinate skin diseases.

ŚUṢKAMŪLAKA TAILA

(Bhāvaprakāśa, Śothādhikāra; 37)

1.	Śuṣkamūlaka	(Pl.)	192 g.
2.	Varṣābhū	(Rt.)	192 g.
3.	Dāru (deva dāru)	(Ht. Wd.)	192 g.
4.	Rāsnā	(Rt. Lf.)	192 g.
5.	Mahauṣadha (śuṇṭhī)	(Rz.)	192 g.
6.	Taila		768 ml.
7.	Water		3.072 l.

Usage: Used externally for massage.

Important therapeutic use: Oedema and colic pain.

ṢAḌBINDU TAILA

(Bhaiṣajyaratnāvalī, Śirorogādhikāra; 49-49½)

1.	Kṛṣṇa tila taila		768 ml.
2.	Ajā paya		3.072 l.
3.	Bhṛṅga rasa (bhṛṅga rāja svarasa)	(Pl.)	3.072 l.
4.	Eraṇḍa mūla	(Rt.)	96 g.

5.	Tagara	(St.)	96 g.
6.	Śatāhvā	(Fl.)	96 g.
7.	Jīvantī	(Rt.)	96 g.
8.	Rāsnā	(Rt./Lf.)	96 g.
9.	Saindhava		96 g.
10.	Bhṛṅga (bhṛṅga rāja)	(Pl.)	96 g.
11.	Viḍaṅga	(Fr.)	96 g.
12.	Madhu yaṣṭī	(Rt.)	96 g.
13.	Viśvauṣadha (śuṇṭhī)	(Rz.)	96 g.

Usage: Used externally for inhalation therapy and massage.
Important therapeutic use: Diseases of nose, teeth, head, eyes and hair.

SAHACARĀDI TAILA

(Aṣṭāṅgahṛdaya, Cikitsāsthāna, Adhyāya 21; 66-67½)

1.	Samūlaśakha sahacara	(Pl.)	2.400 kg.
2.	Bilva	(Rt.)	480 g.
3	Śyonāka	(Rt.)	480 g.
4.	Gambhārī	(Rt.)	480 g.
5.	Pāṭalā	(Rt.)	480 g.
6.	Gaṇikārikā	(Rt.)	480 g.
7.	Śāla parṇī	(Rt.)	480 g.
8.	Pṛśni parṇī	(Rt.)	480 g.
9.	Bṛhatī	(Rt.)	480 g.
10.	Kaṇṭakārī	(Rt.)	480 g.
11.	Gokṣura	(Rt.)	480 g.
12.	Abhīru (śatāvarī)	(Rt.)	2.400 kg.
13.	Water for decoction		49.152 l.
	reduced to		12.288 l.
14.	Sevya (uśīra)	(Rt.)	48 g.
15.	Nakha		48 g.
16.	Kuṣṭha	(Rt.)	48 g.
17.	Hima (śveta candana)	(Ht. Wd.)	48 g.
18.	Elā	(Sd.)	48 g.
19.	Spṛk (spṛkkā)	(Pl.)	48 g.
20.	Priyaṅgu	(Fl.)	48 g.
21.	Nalikā	(Pl.)	48 g.
22.	Ambu (hrībera)	(Rt.)	48 g.

23.	Śilaja (śilā jatu)		48 g.
24.	Lohitā (mañjiṣṭhā)	(St.)	48 g.
25.	Nalada	(Rz.)	48 g.
26.	Loha (agaru)	(Ht. Wd.)	48 g.
27.	Surāhva (deva dāru)	(Ht. Wd.)	48 g.
28.	Kopana (coraka)	(Pl.)	48 g.
29.	Misī	(Fr.)	48 g.
30.	Turuṣka		48 g.
31.	Nata (tagara)	(St.)	48 g.
32.	Kṣira		3.072 l.
33.	Taila		3.072 l.

Usage: Used externally for massage.
Important therapeutic use: Nervous disorders, paralysis agitans and psyzophrenia.

Note: This *taila* is also prepared by boiling for 101 times like *Kṣīrabalā taila*.

SAINDHAVĀDI TAILA

(Bhaiṣajyaratnāvalī, Nāḍīvraṇādhikāra; 31)

1.	Saindhava lavaṇa		
2.	Arka	(Rt.)	192 g.
3.	Marica	(Fr.)	192 g.
4.	Jvalanākhya (citraka)	(Rt.)	192 g.
5.	Mārkava (bhṛṅga rāja)	(Pl.)	192 g.
6.	Haridrā	(Rz.)	192 g.
7.	Dāru haridrā	(St.)	192 g.
8.	Taila		768 ml.
9.	Water		3.072 l.

Usage: Used externally for massage.
Important therapeutic use: Sinus and fistula.

SOMARĀJĪ TAILA

(Bhaiṣajyaratnāvalī, Kuṣṭhādhikāra; 208-208½)

1.	Somarājī (bākucī)	(Sd.)	24 g.
2.	Haridrā	(Rz.)	24 g.

3.	Dāru haridrā	(St.)	24 g.
4.	Sarṣapa	(Sd.)	24 g.
5.	Kuṣṭha	(Rt.)	24 g.
6.	Karañja bīja	(Fr.)	24 g.
7.	Eḍagajā (cakra marda) bīja	(Sd.)	24 g.
8.	Āragvadha patra	(Lf.)	24 g.
9.	Sarṣapa taila		768 ml.
10.	Water		3.072 l.

Usage: Used externally for massage.
Important therapeutic use: Scabies, eczema and psoriasis.

HIṄGUTRIGUṆA TAILA

(Aṣṭāṅgahṛdaya, Cikitsāsthāna, Adhyāya 14; 39)

1.	Hiṅgu	(Exd.)	48 g.
2.	Saindhava (lavaṇaa)		144 g.
3.	Eraṇḍa taila		432 ml.
4.	Rasona rasa	(Bl.)	1.296 l.

Usage: Used externally for massage.
Important therapeutic use: Ascites, phantom tumour and hernia.

Apart from their utility for the Massage therapy, some of these medicated oils are also used for internal administration for the purpose of oleation. Depending upon the exact requirement of the patient, appropriate medicated oil should be selected and necessary changes can be made in these recipes. In traditional practice, several other medicated oils are also used for Massage therapy. The recipes described above are the popular and commonly used ones.

APPENDIX-IV

VEGETABLE DRUGS AND THEIR BOTANICAL NAMES

S. No.	Sanskrit or Popular Name	Important Synonyms	Product/ varieties parts appearing in the formulations	Botanical name
1	2	3	4	5
1.	aklāri (s.y.)	arkarāga		*Lodoicea maldivica* Pers.
2.	Akṣoḍa			*Juglans regia* Linn.
3.	aguru	joṅgaka mālīyaka loha akil (s.y.) kālaloha	kṛṣṇāgaru	*Aquilaria agallocha* Roxb.
4.	agnimantha	jayā muñja (s.y.) gaṇikārikā vaijayanti		*Clerodendrum phlomidis* Linn f.
5.	ajagandhā	paśugandhā		*Gynandropsis gynandra* (Linn.) Briquet.
6.	ajamodā	ajamoda ayamoda dīpyaka ajamoja		*Trachyspermum roxburghianum* (DC.) Sprague
7.	atasī			*Linum usitatissimum* Linn.
8.	atibalā			*Abutilon indicum* (Linn.) Sw.
9.	ativiṣā	aruṇa ghuṇapriyā viṣa vīrā (s.y.) ativiṣa		*Aconitum heterophyllum* Wall.
10.	aparājitā	girikanyā (śvetā)		*Clitoria ternatea* Linn.
11.	apāmārga	mayūra mayūraka kharamañjarī kaṭalāṭi (s.y.) śikhari		*Achyranthes aspera* Linn.
12.	ābhā			*Acacia arabica* Willd.

1	2	3	4	5
13.	ambaṣṭhakī			*Hibiscus sabdariffa* Linn.
14.	amlavetasa	vetasāmla		*Garcinia pedunculata* Roxb.
15.	araluka	kaṭvaṅga		*Ailanthus excelsa* Roxb.
16.	arimeda	irimeda		*Acacia leuocophloea* Willd.
17.	arka	ravi bhānu mandāra tapana		*Calotropis procera* (Ait). R. Br. or *C. gigantea* (Linn.) R.Br. ex Ait.
18.	arjuna	kakubha pārtha śvetavāha		*Terminalia arjuna* W. & A.
19.	aśoka			*Saraca asoca* (Rose) Dc. Wilde
20.	aśvakarṇa			*Dipterocarpus alatus* Roxb.
21.	aśvagandhā	hayagandhā turagagandhā vājigandhā vājigandhika amukkuru (s.y.)		*Withania somnifera* Dunal
22.	aśvattha	pippala		*Ficus religiosa* Linn.
23.	asana	bījaka asanaka pītasāra bījasāra		*Pterocarpus marsupium* Roxb.
24.	asthisaṃhṛta			*Cissus quadrangularis* Linn.
25.	ahiphena	phaṇiphena karuppu (s.y.) nāgaphena		*Papaver somniferum* Linn.
26.	akārakarabha	ākallaka agragrāhi		*Anacyclus pyrethrum* DC.
27.	āḍhakī			*Cajanus cajan* (Linn.) Millsp.
28.	ātmaguptā	kaṇḍūkarī kapikacchu śūkaśiṃbī svayaṃguptā markaṭa svagupta		*Mucuna prurita* Hook.
29.	āmalakī	aṁla āmalaka amṛtaphala haṭha dhātrī nelli (s.y.) nellikka (s.y.)		*Emblica officinalis* Gaertn.

1	2	3	4	5
30.	āmra			*Mangifera indica* Linn.
31.	āmrāta	kapītana ambaka		*Spondias pinnata* Kurz Syn. S. *mangifera* Willd.
32.	āragvadha	kṛtamāla vyādhighāta śampāka śamyāka nṛpadruma kṛtamālaka		*Cassia fistula* Linn.
33.	ārdraka	auṣadha mahauṣadha cuckku (s.y.) nāgara nāgarā nāgaraka viśva viśvabheṣaja śṛṅgavera śṛṅgibera śuṇṭhī viśvā viśvauṣadha		*Zingiber officinale* Rosc.
34.	āsphoṭa			*Hemidesmus indicus* R. Br.
35.	ikṣu	bahurasa	khaṇḍa sitā matsyaṇḍikā śarkarā guḍa sitā sitopala jīrṇaguḍa purāṇaguḍa	*Saccharum officinarum* Linn.
36.	indravāruṇī	gavākṣī indravallī aindrī viśālā indravāruṇikā		*Citrullus colocynthis* Schrad.
37.	īśvarī	nākulī karaleka (s.y.)		*Aristolochia indica* Linn.
38.	uṭiṅgaṇa			*Blepharis edulis* Pers.
39.	utpala	nīlotpala		*Nymphaea stellata* Willd.
40.	udumbara	sadāphala		*Ficus racemosa* Linn.
41.	upakuñcikā	sthūlajīraka upakuñci kāravī suṣavī		*Nigella sativa* Linn.

1	2	3	4	5
42.	uśīra	vīraṇa sevya rāmacca (s.y.) vīraṇaśiphā		*Vetiveria zizanioides* (Linn.) Nash
43.	ṛddhi			*Habenaria intermedia* D. Don
44.	ṛṣabhaka	ṛṣabha		*Microstylis wallichii* Lindl.
45.	eraṇḍa	gandharvahasta vātāri pañcāṅgula citrā urubu rubu uśravūka		*Ricinus communis* Linn.
46.	ervāru	urvāru		*Cucumis melo* var. *utilissimus* Duthie & Fuller
47.	elavāluka	aileya		*Prunus avium* Linn.
48.	kaṅlola	kaṅkolikā cīnoṣaṇa cīnatīkṣṇa kakkola		*Piper cubeba* Linn. f.
49.	kaṭphala	somavalka		*Myrica nagi* Thunb.
50.	kaṭukī	tiktā kaṭabhī tiktarohiṇī tiktaka kaṭurohiṇī kaṭvī rohiṇī kaṭukā kaṭurohiṇī		*Picrorhiza kurroa* Royle ex Benth.
51.	kaṇṭakārī	vyāghrī nidigdhikā kṣudrā kaṇṭakārikā dhāvani nidigdhā dusparśa		*Solanum xanthocarpum* Schrad. & Wendl.
52.	kataka	teṭṭāṃparal (s.y.) katakaphala		*Strychnos potatorum* Linn. f.
53.	kadaṃba			*Anthocephalus cadamba* Miq. A. Rich
54.	kadara			*Acacia suma* Buch-Ham.
55.	kadalī	rambhā		*Musa paradisiaca* Linn.
56.	Kapittha			*Feronia limonia* (Linn.) Swingle

1	2	3	4	5
57.	kamala	abja aravinda padma kalhāra puṇḍarīka puṇḍra āranāla	rakta kamala śveta kamala varaṭa (kamalabīja) padma kanda padma keśara padma kesara kamala kiñjalka mṛṇāla bisa	*Nelumbo nucifera* Gaertn.
58.	kampilla	rajanaka kampillaka		*Mallotus philippinensis* Muell. Arg.
59.	karañja	āvittol (s.y.) karañjaka naktamāla naktāhva ghṛtakarañja		*Pongamia pinnata* (Linn.) Merr.
60.	karavīra	hayamāraka harapriya aśvamāra	śveta karavīra rakta karavīra	*Nerium indicum* Mill.
61.	kariṅkāra			*Carissa carandas* Linn.
62.	karkaṭaśṛṅgī	śṛṅgī viṣāṇi karkaṭa		*Pistacia integerrima* Stew. ex Brandis
63.	karcūra	kaccūra kacoraka karcūra coram (s.y.) gandhapatasā		*Curcuma zedoaria* Rosc.
64.	karpūra	ghanasāraka śaśi indu candraprabhā śītalaraja candra gandhadravya		*Cinnamomum camphora* (Linn.) Nees & Eberm.
65.	kaśeru	kaśeruka		*Scirpus kysoor* Roxb.
66.	kastūrīlatikā			*Hibiscus esculentus* Linn.
67.	kākajaṅghā			*Peristrophe bicalyculata* Nees.
68.	kākatiktā	śatakratulatā uziññа (s.y.)		*Cardiospermum halicacabum* Linn.
69.	kākanāsikā			*Pentatropsis microphylla* W. & A.
70.	kākamācī			*Solanum nigrum* Linn.
71.	kākolī			*Lilium polyphyllum* D. Don

1	2	3	4	5
72.	kāñcanāra	kāñcanāraka		*Bauhinia variegata* Linn.
73.	kāravallī			*Momordica charantia* Linn.
74.	kārpāsa		raktakārpāsa kārpāsāsthi	*Gossypium herbaceum* Linn.
75.	kāśa			*Saccharum spontaneum* Linn.
76.	kirātatikta	kairāta kirātaka kiriyāt (s.y.) bhūnimba kirātatiktaka		*Swertia chirata* Buch. Ham.
77.	kuṅkuma	kāśmīra kāśmīra janma kṣataja vāhlīka		*Crocus sativus* Linn.
78.	kuṭaja	kaliṅga kaliṅgaka vatsa śakra vatsaka	kuṭajatvak indrayava indrabīja vatsabīja	*Holarrhena antidysenterica* Wall.
79.	kunduru	kunduruṣka kundara		*Boswellia serrata* Roxb.
80.	kumārī	kanyā kumārikā	sanniṇāyaka cenniṇāyaka cenyāya sahāsāra kanyāsāra	*Aloe barbadensis* Mill.
81.	kumuda			*Nymphaea alba* Linn.
82.	kuruvikizaṅgu (s.y.)			*Melothria perpusilla* Cogn.
83.	kulattha	khalva vardhipataka		*Dolichos biflorus* Linn.
84.	kuśa			*Desmostachya bipinnata* Stapf
85.	kuṣṭha	āmaya gada ruk pālaka koṭṭam		*Saussurea lappa* C.B. Clarke
86.	kusumbha			*Carthamus tinctorius* Linn.
87.	kūṣmāṇḍa	kūṣmāṇḍaka	kūṣmāṇḍanāḍi	*Benincasa hispida* (Thunb.) Cogn.
88.	kṛṣṇa jīraka	asita jīraka karuñjīraka (s.y.)		*Carum carvi* Linn.
89.	kṛṣṇasārivā	śyāmā		*Cryptolepis buchanani* Roem. & Schult.

1	2	3	4	5
90.	ketakī		ketakīkanda	*Pandanus tectorius* Soland. ex Parkinson or *Pandanus odoratissimus* Roxb.
91.	kokilākṣa	ikṣura ikṣuraka vayalculli (s.y.) kokilākṣī culli (s.y.)		*Asteracantha longifolia* Nees
92.	kodrava			*Paspalum scrobicculatum* Linn.
93.	kozuppā (s.y.)			*Portulaca oleracea* Linn.
94.	kola	kolī badarī	lākṣā kolāsthi	*Zizyphus jujuba* Lam.
95.	kośātakī			*Luffa acutangula* (Linn.) Roxb. var. amara C.B. Clarke
96.	klītaka			*Glycyrrhiza glabra* Linn.
97.	kṣīrakākolī	payasyā kṣīraśuklā		*Fritillaria roylei* Hook.
98.	kṣīravidārī			*Ipomoea digitata* Linn.
99.	khadira	gāyatrī khādira		*Acacia catechu* Willd.
100.	kharjūra			*Phoenix dactylifera* Linn.
101.	gaja pippalī	śreyasī hastipippalī ibhapippalī gajāhvā gajopakulyā		*Scindapsus officinalis* Schott
102.	gandhadūrvā			*Cyperus rotundus* Linn.
103.	gāṅgeru			*Grewia populifolia* Vahl
104.	gambhārī	kāśmarī kāśmarya pītakarohiṇī		*Gmelina arborea* Linn.
105.	guggulu	pura māhiṣākṣa kauśika palaṅkaṣā		*Commiphora mukul* (Hook ex Stocks) Engl.
106.	guḍūcī	amṛtavallī amṛtā chinnodbhavā chinnaruhā somavallī madhuparṇī	guḍūcī sattva	*Tinospora cordifolia* (Willd.) Miers

1	2	3	4	5
		guḍūcikā chinnaroha ciṭṭamṛt (s.y.) amṛta gulūcī		
107.	guñjā	kunni (s.y.)		*Abrus precatorius* Linn.
108.	gokṣura	trikaṇṭaka traikaṇṭaka gokṣuraka śvadaṃṣṭrā ñeriñjil (s.y.)		*Tribulus terrestris* Linn.
109.	gojihva			*Onosma bracteatum* Wall.
110.	granthiparṇī	granthiparṇa granthi granthikā		*Leonotis nepetaefolia* R. Br.
111.	ghoṇṭā			*Zizyphus xylopyra* Willd.
112.	caṇaka	caṇa	caṇakāmla	*Cicer arietinum* Linn.
113.	caṇḍā (corakabheda)			*Angelica archangelica* Linn.
114.	candrikā	āślī (s.y.) jātī		*Lepidium sativum* Linn.
115.	campaka			*Michelia champaca* Linn.
116.	cavya	cavikā		*Piper chaba* Hunter
117.	cāṅgerī			*Oxalis corniculata* Linn.
118.	citraka	agni vahni jvalanākhya kṛśānu hutāśa dahana hutabhuk śikhi		*Plumbago zeylanica* Linn.
119.	ciñcā			*Tamarindus indica* Linn.
120.	cirabilva	cirivilva pūti pūtika pūtigandha		*Holoptelea integrifolia* Planch.
121.	coraka	corakā kopanā corakākhya		*Angelica glauca* Edgw.
122.	chāgakarṇa	śvetasarja		*Vateria indica* Linn.
123.	jaṭāmāṃsī	māṃsī jaṭā nalada jaṭilā		*Nardostachys jatamansi* DC.

1	2	3	4	5
124.	jambū		mahājambū kṣudrajambū	*Syzygium cumini* (Linn.) Skeels
125.	jayanti			*Sesbania sesban* (Linn.) Merr.
126.	jayapāla			*Croton tiglium* Linn.
127.	jalakarṇā			*Lippia nodiflora* Mich.
128.	jātī	mālatī	jātīkusuma jātīpuṣpa	*Jasminum officinale* Linn. Var. grandiflorum Bailey.
129.	jātīphala	jātikośa jātikoṣa jātīsasya jātipatrī jātīdala jātikkā (s.y.) jātīpatra jātīpoṅgāra jātīphalā jātiphala		*Myristica fragrans* Houtt.
130.	jīvaka			*Microstylis muscifera* Ridley.
131.	jīvantī			*Leptadenia reticulata* W. & A.
132.	jyotiṣmatī			*Celastrus paniculatus* Willd.
133.	takkola			*Illicium verum* Hook.f.
134.	tagara	kālānusāri kālānusārikā kālā tagarapādukā nata		*Valeriana wallichii* DC.
135.	tāmalakī	mahīdhātrikā ajjhaḍā		*Phyllanthus niruri* Linn.
136.	tāmracūḍa pādikā			*Adiantum lunulatum* Burm.
137.	tāla		panaviral (s.y.) tālapuṣpakṣāra	*Borassus flabellifer* Linn.
138.	tālamūlī	bhūmitāla		*Curculigo orchioides* Gaertn.
139.	tālīśa	tālīsa tālīsaka	tālīsa patra tālīśa patra	*Abies webbiana* Lindl.
140.	tiniśa			*Ougeinia dalbergioides* Benth.
141.	tintiḍīka	tintriṇī		*Rhus parviflora* Roxb.
142.	timira			*Curcuma longa* Linn.

1	2	3	4	5
143.	tila		taila tilodbhava tila taila sneha tilaja eṇṇa (s.y.) kṛṣṇatila	*Sesamum indicum* Linn.
144.	tumbini			*Lagenaria siceraria* (Mol). Standl.
145.	turuṣka	silhaka		*Liquidambar orientalis* Miller
146.	tulasī	surasā surasa		*Ocimum sanctum* Linn.
147.	tuvaraka			*Hydnocarpus laurifolia* (Dennst.) Sleumer
148.	tejapatra	patra patraka tvakpatra		*Cinnamomum tamala* Nees & Eberm.
149.	tejovatī	tejohva	tumburu	*Zanthoxyhum alatum* Ṛoxb.
150.	trapusa			*Cucumis sativus* Linn.
151.	trāyamāṇā	trāyantī pālanī trāyantikā		*Gentiana kurroo* Royle.
152.	trivṛt	kuṭaraṇā kumbha	śyāma śyāmā trivṛṭā	*Ipomoea turpethum* R. Br.
153.	tvak	coca dārucinī varāṅga		*Cinnamomum zeylanicum* Blume
154.	dantī	nikumha		*Baliospermum montanum* Muell-Arg.
155.	darbha			*Imperata cylindrica* Beauv.
156.	dāḍima			*Punica granatum* Linn.
157.	dāruharidrā	dāru dārvī dāruniśā dārurajanī	añjana rasāñjana	*Berberis aristala* DC.
158.	dugdhikā			*Euphorbia thymifolia* Linn.
159.	dūrvā		śveta dūrvā nīla dūrvā	*Cynodon dactylon* (Linn.) Pers.
160.	devadāru	amaradāru amarakāṣṭha dāru surāhvā		*Cedrus deodara* (Roxb.) Loud.

1	2	3	4	5
		suradruma surāhva suradāru dāruka surapādapa devāhva devadruma devakāṣṭha devāhavaya mahādāru		
161.	dravantī			*Jatropha glandulifera* Roxb.
162.	drākṣā	mṛdvīkā mṛdvīka		*Vitis vinifera* Linn.
163.	droṇapuṣpī	tumbā (s.y.)		*Leucas cephalotes* Spreng.
164.	dhattūra	kanaka unmatta dhustūra dhustūraka dhūrta harapriyā hāṭa hema	svarṇabīja	*Datura metel* Linn.
165.	dhanvayāsa	dhanvayāsaka durālabhā		*Fagonia cretica* Linn.
166.	dhava			*Anogeissus latifolia* Wall.
167.	dhātakī			*Woodfordia fruticosa* Kurz
168.	dhānyaka	kustumburi dhanika dhanyāka dhānyāka vitunnaka		*Coriandrum sativum* Linn.
169.	nandī			*Ficus arnottiana* Miq.
170.	nalikā			*Cinnamomum tamala* Nees & Eberm.
171.	nāgakeśara	keśara kesara nāgapuṣpa nāga nāgakusuma hema ibhakeśara gajakeśara		*Mesua ferrea* Linn.
172.	nāgabalā			*Sida veronicaefolia* Lam.
173.	nāgavallī	ahivallī phaṇivallī	parṇapatra	*Piper betle* Linn.

1	2	3	4	5
174.	nārikela	nālīkera (s.y.) tuṅgadruma madhuphala	pariṇatakerikṣīra	*Cocos nucifera* Linn.
175.	nicula			*Barringtonia acutangula* (Linn.) Gaertn.
176.	nimba	ariṣṭa picumarda nimbaka	sāra	*Azadirachta indica* A. juss.
177.	nimbū	nāraṅga nimbūka nimbu nimbuka jambīra limpāka amla		*Citrus limon* (Linn.) Brum. f.
178.	nirguṇḍī	sinduvāra nirguṇḍikā	nīlanirguṇḍī śvetanirguṇḍī	*Vitex negundo* Linn.
179.	nīlī	nīlikā nīlinī		*Indigofera tinctoria* Linn.
180.	nyagrodha	vaṭa	praroha	*Ficus bengalensis* Linn.
181.	paṭola	karkaśa		*Trichosanthes dioica* Roxb.
182.	pattaṅga			*Caesalpinia sappan* Linn.
183.	padmaka	padmanāluka		*Prunus cerasoides* D. Don
184.	parūṣaka	parūṣa		*Grewia asiatica* Linn.
185.	parpaṭa	parpaṭaka parpaṭī		*Fumaria parviflora* Lam.
186.	pālāśa			*Butea monosperma* (Lam.) Kuntze
187.	paśupāśi			*Myristica malabarica* Lam.
188.	pāṭalāi	pāṭali		*Stereospermum suaveolens* DC.
189.	pāṭalī			*Schrebera swietenioides* Roxb.
190.	pāṭhā			*Cissampelos pareira* Linn.
191.	pāraṅkī			*Garuga pinnata* Roxb.
192.	pāribhadra	pāribhadraka		*Erythrina indica* Lam.
193.	pāṣāṇabheda	aśmabhedaka aśmabhit śilābhit śilābheda kallūrvañcī (s.y.)		*Bergenia ligulata* (Wall.) Engl.

1	2	3	4	5
194.	pippalī	kaṇā kaṇa kṛṣṇā capalā māgadha māgadhī śauṇḍī pippala upakulyā	granthika māgadhiśiphā pippalīmūla granthī	*Piper longum* Linn.
195.	pītacandana	kālīyaka pītasāra haricandana		*Coscinium fenestratum* Colebr.
196.	pīlu	tīkṣṇavṛkṣa	phala	*Salvadora persica* Linn.
197.	pullāni (s.y.)			*Calycopteris floribunda* Lam.
198.	puṣkara	pauṣkara puṣkarākhya puṣkarāhva	puṣkaramūla pauṣkaramūla	*Inula racemosa* Hook. f.
199.	pūga	kramuka ghoṇṭā		*Areca catechu* Linn.
200.	pṛśniparṇī	kalasī guhā dhāvanī		*Uraria picta* Desv.
201.	pezuntol (s.y.)			*Careya arborea* Roxb.
202.	poṭagala			*Typha elephantina* Roxb.
203.	ponnāṅgāṇī (s.y.)			*Alternanthera triandra* Lamk.
204.	prativiṣa			*Aconitum palmatum* D. Don
205.	prapunnāḍa	eḍagajā prapunnāṭa		*Cassia tora* Linn.
206.	prapauṇḍarīka	puṇḍrāhva		*Nelumbo nucifera* Gaertn.
207.	prasāriṇī	saraṇī prasāraṇī talanīli (s.y.) pūtigandhā gandha patrā		*Paederia foetida* Linn.
208.	priyaṅgu	phalinī vanitā priyaṅgukā		*Callicarpa macrophylla* Vahl
209.	priyāla	piyāla		*Buchanania lanzen* Spreng.
210.	plakṣa			*Ficus lacor* Buch.-Ham.
211.	phalgu	malapū (s.y.)		*Ficus hispida* Linn.f.
212.	bakula			*Mimusops elengi* Linn.

1	2	3	4	5
213.	balā	vāṭyālaka		*Sida cordifolia* Linn.
214.	babbūla	bāvarī		*Acacia arabica* Willd.
215.	bākucī	avalguja somarājī		*Psoralea corylifolia* Linn.
216.	bastāntri			*Argyreia speciosa* Sweet
217.	bibhītaka	bibhīta akṣa akṣaka bibhītakī kalivṛkṣa	bibhītakāṅgāra	*Terminalia belerica* Roxb.
218.	bimbī			*Coccinia indica* W. & A.
219.	bilva			*Aegle marmelos* Corr.
220.	bījapūra			*Citrus medica* Linn.
221.	bṛhatgokṣura			*Pedalium murex* Linn.
222.	bṛhatī	cuṇḍā (s.y.) siṃhī		*Solanum indicum* Linn.
223.	bola (hīrābola)			*Commiphora myrrha* (Nees) Engl.
224.	brāhmī			*Bacopa monnieri* (Linn.) Pennel.
225.	bhallātaka	aruṣkara bhallāta		*Semecarpus anacardium* Linn. f.
226.	bhārṅgī	brahmayaṣṭikā bhāraṅgī bhārṅgī		*Clerodendrum serratum* (Linn.) Moon
227.	bhūtika			*Cymbopogon citratus* (DC.) Stapf
228.	bhūtṛṇa			*Cymbopogn jvarankusa* Schult.
229.	bhūrja			*Betula utilis* S. Don
230.	bhṛṅgarāja	kayyonni (s.y.) keśarāja tekarāja bhṛṅga mārkava bhṛṅgaja		*Eclipta alba* Hassk.
231.	mañjiṣṭhā	covvalli (s.y.) asra mañjiṣṭa samaṅgā lohitā lohitayaṣṭikā		*Rubia cordifolia* Linn.
232.	maṇḍūkaparṇī	bhekaparṇikā		*Centella asiatica* (Linn.) Urban

1	2	3	4	5
233.	matsyākṣi	matsyākṣikā mīnākṣī		*Alternanthera sessilis* (Linn.) R. Br.
234.	madana	madanaka	phala	*Randia dumetorum* Lam.
235.	madayantī			*Lawsonia inermis* Linn.
236.	madhusnuhī			*Samilax china* Linn.
237.	madhūka			*Madhuca indica* J.F. Gmel.
238.	madhūrika	miśi miṣi misi		*Foeniculum vulgare* Mill.
239.	marica	vallija vellaja ūṣaṇa ūṣaṇaka		*Piper nigrum* Linn.
240.	masūra			*Lens culinaris* Medic.
241.	mahānimba			*Melia azedarach* Linn.
242.	mahābalā			*Sida rhombifolia* Linn.
243.	mahāmedā			*Polygonatum cirrhifolium* Royle
244.	mātuluṅga			*Citrus medica* Linn.
245.	mādhavī			*Hiptage benghalensis* Kurz
246.	māyakku			*Quercus infectoria* Oliv.
247.	māṣa			*Phaseolus mungo* Linn.
248.	māṣaparṇī	śūrpaparṇī		*Teramnus labialis* Spreng.
249.	mūṇḍitikā	bhūkadamba śrāvaṇī muṇḍī muṇḍīka	mahāśrāvaṇī	*Sphaeranthus indicus* Linn.
250.	mudga			*Phaseolus radiatus* Linn.
251	mudgaparṇī			*Phaseolus trilobus* Ait.
252	muni	munitaru		*Sesbania grandiflora* (Linn.) Pers.
253.	murā			*Selinium tenuifolium* Wall.
254.	musalī	muśalī		*Chlorophytum tuberosum* Baker.
255.	mustā	abda ambuda ghana	āryamuttaṅga (s.y.) bhadramustaka	*Cyperus rotundus* Linn.

1	2	3	4	5
		mustaka jalada ambhodhara balāhaka vārivāha musta payoda	plava	
256.	mūlaka		śuṣkamūlaka mūlakakṣāra	*Raphanus sativus* Linn.
257.	mūrvā	madhusravā madhurasa		*Marsdenia tenacissima* Weight and Arn.
258.	methī			*Trigonella foenum-graceum* Linn.
259.	medā			*Polygonatum cirrhifolium* Royle.
260.	meṣaśṛṅgī			*Gymnema sylvestre* R. Br.
261.	yava		yavāgaraja kṣāra yavakṣāra yāvaśūkaja yavanāla bhasma	*Hordeum vulgare* Linn.
262.	yavānī	dīpyaka yamānī yavānikā yamānikā		*Trachyspermum ammi* (Linn.) Sprague
263.	yavāsaka	yavāsa yāsa yavāṣaka		*Alhagi pseudalhagi* (Bieb.) Desv.
264.	yaṣṭī	yaṣṭikā madhuka madhuyaṣṭī madhu yaṣṭīmadhu yaṣṭīmadhuka yaṣṭyāhva yaṣṭyāhvaya		*Glycyrrhiza glabra* Linn.
265.	rakta candana	raktāṅga kucandana śrīkaṇṭha (s.y.) hima		*Pterocarpus santalinus* Linn. f.
266.	rakta punarnavā	kaṭhilla śophaghnī śothaghnī punarnavā tazutāma (s.y.) varṣābhu		*Boerhaavia diffusa* Linn.

1	2	3	4	5
267.	rāmaśītalikā			*Amaranthus tricolor* Linn.
268.	rāsnā	suvahā surabhi sugandhā aratta (s.y.) yuktā		*Pluchea lanceolata* Oliver & Hiern
269.	rudrākṣa			*Elaeocarpus ganitrus* Roxb.
270.	reṇukā	reṇu kauntī hareṇu reṇuka hareṇuka	bīja	*Vitex agnus-castus* Linn.
271.	rohitaka	rohītaka		*Tecomella undulata* (G. Don) Seem.
272.	rohiṣa	kattṛṇa dhyāma		*Cymbopogon martini* (Roxb.) Wats.
273.	lakuca			*Artocarpus lakoocha* Roxb.
274.	lakṣmaṇā			*Solanum xantho-carpum* Schrad & Wendl. (white variety)
275.	lajjālu	samaṅgā varākrāntā		*Mimosa pudica* Linn.
276.	latākarañja			*Caesalpinia crista* Linn.
277.	lavaṅga	lavaṅgaka devapuṣpa devapuṣpaka karyāmpu (s.y.) varāla karāmpu		*Syzygium aromaticum* (Linn.) Merr. & L.M. Perry
278.	laśuna	rasona ulli (s.y.)		*Allium sativum* Linn.
279.	lāṅgalī	kalikāri lāṅgalakī		*Gloriosa superba* Linn.
280.	lāmajjaka	lāmajja		*Cymbopogon jwarancusa* Schult.
281.	lodhra	rodhra tiriṭa pāccoṭṭi (s.y.)	śābara lodhra paṭṭikā lodhra	*Symplocos racemosa* Roxb.
282.	vacā	ṣaḍgranthā ugrā ugragandhā vayambu (s.y.)		*Acorus calamus* Linn.
283.	vāñjulā			*Salix caprea* Linn.
284.	vanya jīraka			*Centratherum anthel-minticum* (Willd.) Kuntze

1	2	3	4	5
285.	vatsanābha	amṛta viṣa vajranāga sthāvaraviṣa vatsanāgaka		*Aconitum chasmanthum* (Stapf ex Holmes)
286.	varuṇa	varaṇa		*Crataeva nurvala* Buch.-Ham.
287.	varṣābhu			*Trianthema portulacastrum* Linn.
288.	vasuka			*Osmanthus fragrans* Lowr.
289.	vārāhi			*Dioscorea bulbifera* Linn.
290.	vāsā	vāsaka vṛṣa siṃhavadanā vṛṣaka āṭarūṣa		*Adhatoda vasica* Nees
291.	vijayā	bhaṅgā indrāśana trailokyavijayā		*Cannabis sativa* Linn.
292.	viḍaṅga	jantughna kṛmighna kṛmihara kṛmiripu vella	sāra	*Embelia ribes* Burm. f.
293.	vidārī	vidāri vidārikā	vidāricūrṇa vidārikanda	*Pueraria tuberosa* DC.
294.	viṣamuṣṭi	viṣatindu viṣataru kucila viṣamuṣṭikā		*Strychnos nuxvomica* Linn.
295.	viralā			*Diospyros tomentosa* Roxb.
296.	vṛkṣāmla			*Garcinia indica* Chois.
297.	vṛddhadāruka	vṛddhadāru vṛddhadāraka vṛddhadāra		*Ipomoea petaloidea* Choisy.
298.	vṛddhi			*Habenaria intermedia* D. Don
299.	vṛścikālī			*Tragia involucrata* Linn.
300.	vaṃśa		vaṃśalocanā śubhā tugākṣīrī tvakṣīrī vasu tugā vaṃśajā vaṃśarocanā kūvaūral (s.y.)	*Bambusa bambos* Druce

1	2	3	4	5
301.	śaṅkhapuṣpī	śaṅkhapuṣpa		*Convolvulus pluricaulis* Choisy.
302.	śaṅkhinī			*Calonyction muricatum* (Linn.) G. Don
303.	śaṭī	śaṭhī		*Hedychium spicatum* Ham. ex. Smith
304.	śaṇa			*Crotalaria juncea* Linn.
305.	śatapatrikā	taruṇī śatapatra	gulābarka himāmbha	*Rosa centifolia* Linn.
306.	śatāvarī	abhīru nārāyaṇī varī		*Asparagus racemosus* Willd.
307.	śatāhvā	śatapuṣpā		*Anethum sowa* Kurz.
308.	śara			*Saccharum munja* Roxb.
309.	śāka			*Tectona grandis* Linn. f.
310.	śakhoṭaka			*Streblus asper* Lour.
311.	śāla		rāla śālasāra suradhūma ceñcalya (s.y.) ceñcaliya	*Shorea robusta* Gaertn. f.
312.	śālaparṇī	aṃśumatī sthirā		*Desmodium gangeticum* DC.
313.	śālī		raktaśāli dhānya āranāla tuṣa lāja lājā kāñjikā taṇḍulāmbu dhānyāmla śukta nīra	*Oryza sativa* Linn.
314.	śālmalī	moca mocāhva	mocarasa	*Salmalia malabarica* Schott & Endl.
315.	śigru	śobhāñjana bahala	śigrūdbhava	*Moringa pterygosperma* Gaertn.
316.	śirīṣa	bhaṇḍī		*Albizzia lebbeck* Benth.
317.	śiṃśapā			*Dalbergia sissoo* Roxb.
318.	śṛṅgāṭaka	śṛṅgāṭa		*Trapa bispinosa* Roxb.
319.	śuṇṭhī (dried form)			*Zingiber officinale* Rosc.

1	2	3	4	5
320.	śaileya	śaileyaka		*Parmelia perlata* Ach.
321.	śyonāka			*Oroxylum indicum* Vent.
322.	śveta candana	ekāṅgī hima śrīkhaṇḍa candana śrīgandha		*Santalum album* Linn.
323.	śveta jīraka	ajājī ajāji jīraka		*Cuminum cyminum* Linn.
324.	śveta punarnavā	vṛścīva vṛścīraka		*Boerhaavia verticilata* Poir.
325.	śveta sārivā	anantā gopasutā gopī naṅnāri (s.y.) sāriva		*Hemidesmus indicus* R. Br.
326.	saptaparṇa	saptacchada saptaparṇī saptāhvā		*Alstonia scholaris* R. Br.
327.	saptalā	carmasāhvā sātalā		*Euphorbia dracunculoides* Lam.
328.	sarala		śrīvāsa śrīnivāsaka	*Pinus roxburghii* Sargent
329.	sarja		sarjarasa	*Vateria indica* Linn.
330.	sarṣapa		gaura sarṣapa siddhārtha kaṭu taila	*Brassica campestris* Linn. var. rapa (Linn.) Hartm.
331.	sahacara	bāṇa kuraṇṭaka sairīyā koraṇḍa koraṇḍaka		*Barleria prionitis* Linn.
332.	sahadevī			*Vernonia cinerea* Lees.
333.	sūkṣmailā	truṭi tuṭī elā elāsūkṣma		*Elettaria cardamonum* Maton.
334.	sūraṇa	sūraṇaka		*Amorphophallus campanulatus* (Roxb.) BL.
335.	somavallī			*Sarcostemma brevistigma* W.A.
336.	sthūla elā	bhadrā bhadrailā elā		*Amomum subulatum* Roxb.
337.	sthauṇeya			*Taxus baccata* Linn.

1	2	3	4	5
338.	snuhī	sudhā vajra snuk kallī (s.y.)	snugyagra	*Euphorbia nerifolia* Linn.
339.	spṛkkā	spṛk		*Schizachyrum exile* (Hochst) Stapf
340.	sruvavṛkṣa			*Flacourtia indica* Merr.
341.	svarṇakṣirī			*Euphorbia thomsoniana* Boiss.
342.	svarṇapatrī			*Cassia angustifolia* Vahl
343.	hapuṣā	kapotavaṅkā havuṣā		*Juniperus communis* Linn.
344.	haridrā	rajanī niśā niśi rātri kṣaṇada doṣā paimañjal (s.y.)		*Curcuma longa* Linn.
345.	harītakī	abhayā kāyasthā śivā pathyā vijayā abhayā		*Terminalia chebula* Retz.
346.	hiṅgu	rāmaṭha sahasravedhi vedhī		*Ferula foetida* Regel.
347.	hiṅgupatrī			*Ferula jaeschkeana* Vatke.
348.	hiṃsrā	kārtoṭṭi (s.y.)		*Capparis spinosa* Linn.
349.	hṛddhātrī			*Smilax china* Linn.
350.	haṃsapadī	tripādī haṃsapādī		*Adiantum lunnulatum* Burm.
351.	hrīvbera	ambu ambhas udaka udīcya jala toya bālā bālaka vāri hiruberaka iruveli (s.y.) bāla		*Coleus vettiveroides* C. Jacob.

(Based on the Ayurvedic Formulary of India: Pt.I., 1st edn.; Pub. Ministry of Health & F.P., New Delhi, 1978).

BIBLIOGRAPHY

Agniveśa, *Carakasaṃhitā*, ed. Jādavaji Trikamji Āchārya, Pub. Bombay: Nirnaya Sagar Press, 3rd ed., 1941.

Bhāvamiśra *Bhāvaprakāśa*, ed. Brahma-śaṅkara Śāstrī, Pub. Vārāṇasī: Chaukhambha Sanskrit Series, 1956.

Chopra, R.N. *et. al. Glossary of Indian Medicinal Plants*, Pub. New Delhi: Council of Scientific & Industrial Research, Rep. 1986.

Dash, Bhagwan, *Meteria Medica of Ayurveda based on Madanapāla's Nighaṇṭu*, Pub. New Delhi: B. Jain Publishers, 1991.

Govindadāsa, *Bhaiṣajyaratnāvalī*, ed. Narendranātha Mitra, *et. al.* Varanasi: Motilal Banarasidas, 1963.

Kaladi Basava, *Śivatattva ratnākaraḥ*, ed. Su. Narayanasvami Śāstrī, Pub. Mysore: Prācyavidyā-saṃśodhanālaya, Mysore University, 1964.

Kaladi Basava, *Ayurvedic Formulary of India*, Pt. I, Pub. New Delhi: Ministry of Health & F.W., 1st ed. 1978.

Mooss, N.S., *Ayurvedic Treatments of Kerala*, Pub. Kottayam: Vaidyasarathi Press 3rd ed., 1983.

Mulugu, Ramalingaya, *Yogaratnākaraḥ*, ed. Brahmaśaṅkara Śāstrī, Pub. Vārānasī: Chaukhambha Samskṛta Samsthāna, 4th ed., 1988.

Mulugu, Ramalingaya, *Vaidyayogaratnāvalī*, ed. Visveswara Sastri, Pub. Adyar, Madras: Madras State Indian Medical Practitioners Co-operative Pharmacy, 1966.

Śārṅgadhara, *Śārṅgadharasaṃhitā*, ed. Parśurāma Śāstrī, Pub. Bombay: Nirnaya Sagar Press, 2nd ed., 1962.

Śārṅgadhara, *Sahasrayogam*, ed. Vetāyudha Kurup, Pub. Quilon: Srirama Vilasam Press, 1963.

Suśruta, *Suśrutasaṃhitā*, ed. Jadavaji Trikamji Acharya and Narayana Rama Acharya, Rep. Varanasi: Chaukhambha Orientalia, 1980.

Vāgbhaṭa, *Aṣṭāṅgahṛdaya*, ed. Āṇṇā Moreśvara Kunṭe & Kṛṣṇaśāstrī Navare, Rep. Varanasi: Kṛṣṇadāsa Academy, 1982.

INDEX

abhyaṅga (massage), 19
aga(u)ru (Aquilaria agallocha), 35, 43
agnis, 17
ajājī (Nigella sativa), 35
āma (uncooked food), 28
āmalakī (Emblica officinalis), 68, 72
āmrātaka (spondias pinnata), 42
anemia, 81
animal fat, 39
anorexia, 34, 68, 81, 82
anuvāsana therapy, 28, 29
anxiety, 73
apāmārga (Achyranthes aspera), 40
apatarpaṇa (depleting therapy), 18
appearance of wrinkles, 57
āragvadha (Cassia fistula), 35, 40, 41
Ārdrā constellation, 26
arjuna (Terminalia arjuna), 35, 48
arka (Calotropis procera), 78
arteriosclearosis, 21
asana (Pterocarpus marsupium), 48
āsanas (yogic physical postures), 76
Aṣṭāṅga hṛdaya, 21, 32
Aṣṭāṅga saṅgraha, 25
asthi (bone tissue), 32
atasī (Linum usitatissimum), 42
āyuś (longevity), 21, 23
bāhya snehana (external oleation therapy), 18
bākucī (Psoralea corylifolia), 35, 42
balā (Sida rhombifolia), 45, 50, 65, 66
Bālā or *hrībera (Coleus vettiveroides)*, 35
baldness, 30, 57
bhallātaka (Semecarpus anacardium), 41, 43
bibhītaka (Terminalia belerica), 43
bilva (Aegle marmelos), 42
bitter gourd, 72
black gram (flour), 60, 70, 78
black pepper, 72
black pigmentation of the face, 81
blood-letting therapy, 28, 81
bola (Commiphora myrrha), 35
bone-marrow (both white and red varieties), 37, 38
brāhmī or *kapotavaṇkā* or *suvarcalā*, 42
broken bones, 38
bronchial asthma, 73
burning sensation, 58, 66, 68
  in the feet, 31
butter, 37, 39, 68, 72, 74
buter-milk, 39, 61, 62, 68
Cakramarda (Cassia tora), 35
Calculus in urinary tract, 42
Camphor, 66
Candana (Santalum album), 35
Caraka saṃhitā, 25, 28
cardiac pain, 80, 82
cataract, 68, 70
chick-pea (flour), 55, 60, 78
chronic fever, 66
chronic insomnia, 68
chronic rheumatism, 57
coated tongue, 73
coconut, 66
coconut water, 66
colic pain, 80
contractions in the musculature, 82
convulsions, 82
coriander, 71, 74
cow's ghee, 58, 65, 74
cow's milk, 51, 65, 66, 68
cracking in the soles of the feet, 32
cramps in the calf-muscles, 80
cream, 72
cumin-seeds, 71, 74
dantī (Baliospermum montanum), 40
dārḍhya (sturdiness), 21, 24
dāru haridrā (Berberis aristata) 35
deafness, 31, 82
delirium, 66
devadālī (Luffa echinata), 40
deva dāru (Cedrus deodara), 35
dhāmārgava or *mahākoṣātakī (Luffa cylindrica)*, 40
dhānyaka (Coriandrum sativum), 35
dhārā therapy, 68
dhattūra (Datura metel), 78
dhātus (tissue elements composing the body), 17, 23
diabetes, 57
disfiguration of the skin, 34
distension of the lower abdomen, 80
doṣas, 17, 40

dravantī (Croton tiglium), 40
drowsiness, 34, 73, 83
dṛṣṭi (eye-sight), 22
dṛṣṭi prasāda, 21
dry-ginger, 71, 74
dryness, 32
dryness of mouth, 70, 82
nose, 70
throat, 82
dugdha dhārā, 61, 66
dūrvā (Cynodon dactylon), 26
dyspnoea, 81
dysuria, 80
earache, 31, 38
elā (Amomum subulatum), 35
emaciation, 82
emetic therapy, 40, 81
epileptic fits, 60
eraṇḍa (Ricinus communis), 40, 77
ervāruka (Cucumis utilissimus), 41
erysipelas, 59, 81
excessive sweating, 34
exhaustion, 82
eye-diseases, 82
facial paralysis, 70, 81
fainting, 59, 83
fasting therapy, 81
fatigue, 32, 59, 68, 73, 81
fever, 59, 76, 81
filling the ears with oil, 31
flatulence, 73
flour of black gram, 69
fomentation therapy, 80, 81
foul-breath, 73
fruit-juice, 74
Gandharvahastādi kaṣāya, 74
Gāyatrī mantra, 56
ghee, 37, 39, 72, 74
ghṛta (ghee), 37
ghṛta dhārā, 65
giddiness, 21, 31, 66, 68, 73, 82
gout, 56, 73
granthi parṇī (Angelica glauca), 35
green gram (flour), 55, 78
ground-nut oil, 72
guggulu (Commiphora mukul), 35
haemorrhage, 59
hair-fall, 30
haridrā (Curcuma longa), 35
harītakī (Terminalia chebula), 42
headache, 30, 31, 38, 68, 70, 73, 80, 81, 83
head-diseases, 70
head-massage, 29, 30
heart-diseases, 21, 68, 73, 76, 82, 83
hemicrania, 81
hemiplegia, 73
hiccup, 81
high blood pressure, 21, 22, 57, 73, 76
hrībera (Coleus vettiveroides), 35
human (breast) milk, 66
ikśvāku or *kaṭu tumbī*, 40
indrāyaṇa (Citrullus colocynthis), 40
iṅgudī (Balanites agyptica), 41, 43
inhalation (therapy), 28, 80
insanity, 66
insomnia, 56, 61
instability in gait, 68
itching, 34
jarā (ageing process), 21
jaṭāmāṃsī (Nardostachys jatamansi), 35
Jyeśṭhā constellation, 26
jyotiṣmatī (Celastrus paniculatus), 41, 42
kampillaka (Mallotus philippinensis), 40, 41
kapha, 17, 22, 25, 34, 37-39
(phlegm), 60
kapha-alleviating drugs, 38
kaphaja diseases, 70
kapittha (Feronia limonia), 41
kapotavaṅkā (Bacopa monnieri), 42
karañja (Pongamia pinnata), 41, 78
karkandhu (Zizyphus nummularia), 35
karkāru (Cucurbita maxima), 41
karkaṭī or *ervāruka (Cucumis utilissimus)*, 41
karṇapūraṇa (filling the ears with oil), 29, 31
kaṭu tumbī (Lagenaria siceraria), 40, 42
kāya seka, 58
khadira (Acacia catechu), 48
khichri (thin gruel of rice and moong dal), 74
kirāta tikta (Swertia chirata), 41
koṣāmra (Schleichera oleosa), 40
kośātakī (Luffa cylindrica), 40
kuśmāṇḍa (Cucurbita pepo), 41
kuṣṭha (Saussurrea lappa), 34
(obstinate skin diseases including leprosy), 41
kuṭaja (Holarrhena antidysenterica), 40
latākarañja (Caesalpinia crista), 41
lavaṅga (Syzygium aromaticum), 35
laxative, 40
leucoderma, 42
lock-jaw, 31
lodhra (Symploeos racemosa), 35
Madanapāla's *nighaṇṭu*, 39
madanaphala (Randia dumetorum), 40, 43
mādhavi (Hiptage benghalensis), 42

mathūka (Madhuca indica), 42
madirā (a type of wine), 80
mahākoṣātakī (Luffa cylindrica), 40
majjā (bone-marrow), 32, 37, 38
mala(s) (waste products), 17, 79
malaise, 80, 82, 83
mālatī (Aganosma dichotoma), 78
māṃsa (muscle-tissue), 32
mañjiṣṭhā (Rubia cordifolia), 42
mantras (sacred incantation), 78
massage over the soles of feet, 32
mātrās (seconds), 32, 33
mātuluṅga (Citrus medica), 41
medas (fat tissue), 32, 38
medicated enema, 28, 80, 81
meśa śṛṅgī (Pistacia intergerrima), 40
migraine, 73
milk, 39, 61, 62, 74
minor skin-disorders, 43
moca (Salmalia malabarica), 42
moong (dal), 72, 74
musta (Cyperus rotundus), 34, 68
mustard oil, 25, 27
mūtrasaṅga (anuria), 41
nāga kesara (Mesua ferrea), 35
nārikela (Cocus nucifera), 42
nasya (therapy), 28, 29
navara, (Oryza picta), 45
navarakizhi, 45, 62
nervous disorders, 22, 42
nervous irritability, 73
neuralgia, 76
neurasthenia, 76
nilinī (Indigofera tinctoria), 40
nimba (Azadirachta indica), 35, 42
nirūha therapy, 28
nīvāra or *navara (Oryza picta)*, 45
numbness, 32, 82
obesity, 28
obstacles in the functioning of the heart and lungs, 81
oedema, 81
offensive perspiration, 73
oil (medicated), 39, 61, 62, 72
oil of oil seeds, 39
ojas, 37
oleation of head, 69
oleation therapy, 19, 25, 27, 81
olive oil, 72
Oṃ, 56, 78
osteo-arthritis, 21, 56
pādābhyaṅga (massage in the soles of the feet), 29, 32
padmaka (Prunus cerasoides), 35
pain, 21
in abdomen, 81
in bladder, 80
in joints, 59
in phallus, 80
in testicles, 80
paittika diseases, 69
palāśa (Butea monosperma), 40
panasa (Artocarpus heterophyllus), 42, 78
pañcakarma (five specialised therapies), 28
paralysis agitans, 21, 66
Parkinson's disease, 21, 73
paṭola (Trichosanthes cucumerina), 41
pāyasam, 45
phantom tumour, 83
physical exercise, 26
pīlu (Salvadora persica), 41
Piṇḍa sveda, 45, 48
pīta dāru (Berberis aristata), 43
pitta, 17, 22, 25, 37-39, 42, 57, 60
pizhichil, 58
pouring oil over the head, 60
prāṇāyāma (breathing exercises), 76
premature greying of hair, 30, 57, 68
priyāla (Buchanania lanzan), 42
priyaṅgu (Callicarpa macrophylla), 43
process of ageing, 57
prolapse of uterus, 38
pruritus, 81
psoriasis, 73,
psyzophrenia, 61
punnāga (Calophyllum inophyllum), 35
purgation therapy, 28, 81
puśkara mūla (Inula racemosa), 35
puṣṭi (nourishment of the body or of tissue elements), 21, 23
raktaja diseases (diseases caused by the vitiation of blood), 69
rakta-mokṣaṇa (blood-letting therapy), 28, 29
rasa (Chyle & plasma), 37, 38
refraction errors of eyes, 30
retention of faeces, 80, 81
flatus, 80, 81
urine, 80, 81
rheumatic arthritis, 73
rheumatoid arthritis, 73
rhinitis, 82
rice, 74
ringworm, 43
Rubbing the body with powders, 36
saindhava (rock-salt), 35
ṣali rice *(Oryza sativa)*, 80
śaṅkhinī (Calonyction muricatum), 40
saṅkrānti days (when the sun moves

from one zordiac sign to the other), 26
santarpaṇa (nourishing therapy), 18
saptalā (Acacia concinna), 40
sarala (Pinus roxburghii), 35, 43
sarja rasa (Vateria indica), 35
sarśapa (Brassica compestris), 35, 41, 42
śaṣṭika (Oriza picta), 45
śatāvarī (Asparagus racemosa), 66
sciatica, 32
sesame oil, 27, 39, 58, 65
śigru (Moringa pterigosperma), 77
śiṃṣapā (Dalbergia sissoo), 43
śirīśa (Albizzia lebbeck), 78
śirobasti (elimination of *doṣas* from the head), 30, 69, 70
śirobhyaṅga (head-massage), 29, 30
śirodhārā, 61
śirovirecana (elimination of *doṣas* from the head), 40
skin-diseases, 41, 81
sleeplessness, 65, 68, 70, 73
śleṣmā (phlegm), 22
śleṣmāntaka, 42
smoking therapy, 81
sneha (fatty substances like oil, ghee, etc), 27
snehana (oleation therapy), 18, 19, 37
sneha pāna (drinking oil, ghee, etc.), 19
soap-nut, 59, 78
śobhāñjana (Moringa pterygosperma), 40
śrāddha (offerings made to dead ancestors), 26
śrama (exhaustion), 21, 22
śrāvaṇa constellation, 26
stambhana (therapy which inhibits unnatural secretion), 18
stiffness of the body, 21
in the joints, 56
suppositories, 80, 81
sūraṅa (Amorphophallus companulatus), 72
surasā (Ocomum sanctum), 78
Sūryavallī (Gynandropis gynandra), 40
Suśruta saṃhitā, 17, 29
suvarcalā, 42
svapna (sleep), 21, 24
swelling in the joints, 56
śyonāka (Oroxylum indicum), 43
taila (oil), 37, 38
taila dhārā, 61, 62, 65, 66
taila droṇi, 57
takra dhārā, 61, 68
tāla (Borassus flabelliger), 42
tila (Sesanum indicum), 35
tilvaka (Symplcos racemosa), 40
tinitus, 31
tobacco, 75
torticolis, 31, 81
trapusa (Cucumis satives), 41
trembling in the body, 82
tremor, 81, 82
tub-bath, 80
tuberculosis, 76
tulasī (Ocimum sanctum), 35
tumbī (Lagenaria siceraria), 41
typhoid fever, 66
udgharśaṇa (rubbing the body with powder of drugs), 36
udvartana (unction), 34
ulcer-healing, 41
unconsciousness, 66
unction, 34
urge for breathing, 83
defecation, 80
drinking liquids, 82
emesis, 81
eructation, 81
hunger, 82
micturation, 80
passing flatus, 81
seminal discharge, 80
sleep, 82
sneezing, 81
weeping, 82
yawning, 82
urinary disorders, 41
urticaria, 59, 81
Uttarā phālguni constellation, 26
Vāgbhaṭa, 21, 32
Vājigandhā (Withania somnifera), 35
vamana therapy, 28
vasā (muscle fat), 37, 38
vāta (nervous system), 21
vāta (one of the three *doṣas*), 22
vāta roga (diseases caused by the vitiation of *vāta*), 22
vātika diseases (diseases caused by the vitiation of *vāyu*), 69
vāyu, 17, 22, 25, 27, 34, 36, 37, 39, 42, 57, 60, 81-83.
vegarodha (suppression of natural urges), 79
viḍaṅga (Embelia ribes), 40
virecana (therapy purgation therapy), 28
vomiting, 59, 68
vyavāyin, 39
weakness of vertibral coloum, 21
yagavāhin, 38
yoghurt, 39